50 REAL

LAW SCHOOL

PERSONAL STATEMENTS

And Everything You Need to Know to Write Yours

By **jdMission** Senior Consultants

MANHATTAN PREP
PUBLISHING

50 Real Law School Personal Statements
And Everything You Need to Know to Write Yours

Published by Manhattan Prep Publishing, Inc.
138 W 25th St, 7th Floor
New York, NY 10001
www.manhattanprep.com/publishing

ISBN-10: 1-941234-54-2
ISBN-13: 978-1-941234-54-9
eISBN: 978-1-941234-56-3

Layout Design by Derek Frankhouser and Cathy Huang
Cover Design by Carly Schnur

About jdMission

jdMission's elite admissions consulting services give law school applicants a competitive edge as they strive to secure a place in the school of their dreams. All our consultants are graduates of top law schools as well as profoundly experienced writers and editors, and are devoted to helping applicants identify and communicate the distinct characteristics that will distinguish them from the rest of the applicant pool. With one-on-one guidance and assistance, we work tirelessly to help our clients maximize their chances of admission and achieve their law school goals.

TABLE OF CONTENTS

INTRODUCTION

Maybe you have taken the LSAT, or maybe you have not. Maybe you have finished college, or maybe you have not. Maybe you are making a career change, or maybe law will be your very first career. Regardless of who you are and your current situation, if you have decided to apply to law school, you are definitely facing the challenge of writing an effective personal statement.

First, the good news: because the personal statement question or prompt is fairly standard from one JD program to the next, you will likely be able to use your final essay to apply to multiple schools. Your task is to demonstrate, in a two- to four-page composition, why your target law school should accept you into its next incoming class of aspiring JDs.

Consider these recent personal statement prompts from the applications of several "top ten" law schools:

> **Law School 1:** Candidates ... are required to submit a personal essay or statement supplementing required application materials. Such a statement may provide the Admissions Committee with information regarding such matters as: personal, family, or educational background; experiences and talents of special interest; reasons for applying to law school as they may relate to personal goals and professional expectations; or any other factors that you think should inform the Committee's evaluation of your candidacy for admission. This statement should be printed on a supplementary sheet or two and should be returned to the Law School with other application materials.

> **Law School 2:** An applicant may write a double-spaced personal statement on any subject of importance that he or she feels will assist the Admissions Committee in its decision. There is no minimum/maximum length.

Law School 3: The Personal Statement provides an opportunity for you to present yourself, your background, your ideas, and your qualifications to the Admissions Committee. Please limit your statement to two pages using a minimum of 11-point font, 1-inch margins, and double spacing. Please refer to the Statement Form for more information. Attach your statement to the Statement Form when submitting on paper.

You get the idea.

Of course, you will encounter some exceptions and variations. Some schools have relatively short page limits, while others have no page limits at all. Some schools ask specifically what you will contribute to their program or what draws you to it rather than others. But most admissions committees generally want the same thing, which is for you to tell them something about yourself that is not already demonstrated by the other elements of your application. In short, what can you convey about yourself as an individual who is more complex and three-dimensional than a resumé or GPA or LSAT score? You must show the schools that you are someone they want in their classrooms, among their students, and eventually, on their roster of alumni.

This book is designed to help you write the best personal statement you can (which you can then tailor, if necessary, to particular schools). The best part is that our guidance and tips are not presented to you in a vacuum. We do not simply say, "Show rather than tell!" and then leave you on your own to figure out what that means. We include here a total of 50 personal statement reviews discussing numerous facets of the essay-crafting process, from drafting to the final revision. Each lesson is derived from an actual personal statement that in some way embodies the lesson we want to impart—either it illustrates the mistake we are advising you to avoid, or it demonstrates a technique we are encouraging you to employ. A jdMission Senior Consultant offers a thorough critique of each essay, including a First Impression based solely on the personal statement's first paragraph, an enumeration of the essay's particular Strengths and Weaknesses, and a Final Assessment of the statement as a whole.

Start by reading through a few essays and their critiques. Before long, you should begin to develop a sense of what a personal statement is and the kinds of mistakes applicants commonly make in writing them. Once that happens, try this: read the first paragraph of a personal statement, determine *your* first impression, and then skip ahead to read the jdMission Senior Consultant's First Impression in the review. Was your judgment similar to that of the consultant? If not, how did it differ?

Then, as you read through the rest of the essay, do so with a critical eye. Ask yourself repeatedly what you think of it. If you were an admissions officer, how would you feel about the essay and the candidate who wrote it? Is the applicant trying too hard to sound smart or to sell a sob story that does not ring true? Do you find yourself wanting to be friends with her or to hire him as your attorney someday? Do you lose interest midway through and think about skipping ahead to the next essay? As you go, jot down your thoughts in the margins or on a separate sheet of paper.

When you reach the jdMission review of the essay you just read, ask yourself these questions: What did you notice that the critique does not mention? What does the review reference that you missed? If your opinion differs greatly from the jdMission consultant's, that could be a valuable indicator for you. It could mean that you are susceptible to making the same mistake(s) that the candidate who authored that particular essay did, so you should pay particular attention to the advice provided in the accompanying review. Of course, you could simply disagree with the consultant's opinion, but keep in mind that the observations and guidance in these reviews are based on our many years of professional experience in this area, and we are being entirely frank about these essays' weaknesses and merits for your benefit.

If you have already drafted your essay and are in the revising stage, consider scanning the table of contents for specific tips that may pertain to you and/or consult the index to learn which reviews touch on writing/elements that may be giving you trouble. This way, you can target your reading so that it is tailored to your personal revision needs. However, we would encourage you, if time allows, to read through all the chapters, because you may find a suggestion or idea that you might not have otherwise considered but that may be key in taking your personal statement to the next level.

Whether you have yet to write a single word or have completed a thousand drafts, you will likely find that simply by reading other candidates' essays and deciding for yourself which elements work and which do not, you will be better equipped to make your own personal statement shine.

And finally, a suggestion for all readers: as you read through this book, mark your favorite essays. Bookmark also the ones that confused you, bored you, or left you wondering which frozen pizza you should have for dinner. Taking note of the boring essays will allow you to use them as comparisons against your own. The danger is that you might inadvertently write a statement that is similar to the ones you find bland or dull; because we do not typically bore ourselves, we are not always aware of when we are boring others. So use the boring essays as a yardstick by which to measure your drafts. Likewise, use your favorite essays as inspiration and models for your writing, noting what you like about them—such as their style, syntax, or structure—and replicate those elements in your own essay.

We need to clarify one important thing before we begin: although we have changed or removed any identifying details from these statements, we have not otherwise edited the personal statements, in the interest of maintaining the integrity and authenticity of this project. Any grammatical errors that appear in the essays are attributable to the candidate authors and illustrate the importance of having someone (or multiple someones) proofread your work before you submit it. Wherever such errors are egregious, we have addressed them in the critiques.

Note also that only one of the statements reviewed here (#20) is a response to the "Yale 250" essay—Yale Law School's infamous 250-word secondary (required) essay, which is equal to approximately one page, double-spaced. Many applicants to Yale Law School find this word limit tremendously challenging, so we have included this example to offer our best advice on managing it. As we note in the critique, though, our guidance should be of assistance to anyone struggling with *any* word limit, not just a painfully restrictive one.

We hope that you find this book helpful in whatever way best suits your particular needs and that it inspires you to think more creatively, critically, and attentively about how you present yourself in your law school personal statement. Applying to law school is not just a numbers game—we at jdMission can offer a wealth of unlikely success stories to prove it. Go show the admissions committees what you have to offer!

Sincerely,

jdMission Senior Consultants

JD Applicants'
Top Ten Essay Mistakes

1. Failing to adequately reflect on experiences.

2. Choosing a theme that is not as smart as it could be.

3. Using clichés and nonspecific language.

4. Missing opportunities to engage the reader.

5. Regurgitating one's resumé.

6. Claiming an epiphany or realization without describing what it was.

7. Making grammatical errors.

8. Employing wacky gimmicks.

9. Being wordy.

10. Ending with vague or grandiose generalizations.

NOTE

Although we have changed or removed any identifying details from the personal statements reviewed in this book, we have not otherwise edited the original essays, in the interest of maintaining the integrity and authenticity of this project. Any grammatical errors that appear in the essays are attributable to the candidate authors and illustrate the importance of having someone (or multiple someones) proofread your work before you submit it. Wherever such errors are egregious, we have addressed them in the critiques.

PERSONAL STATEMENT 1

Reflect rather than just reciting.

I have always been really interested in the rhythm of words, the musicality of communication. Immediate, impassioned speech—usually short and sweet—gets the point across better than Chaucer or Joyce. I studied dance from a young age and, for a short while, to my mother's chagrin, played the drums.

When I was living in Brooklyn just after graduation from undergrad with a lovely-if-useless poetry degree, I attended a meeting with a friend that introduced me to the idea of eminent domain. A new stadium, along with a commercial and residential complex, was being erected in what seemed like the middle of the street, in a sunken railway line where old, underused subway trains landed when they had no where else to go. I later learned the site was called the "Pacific Yards," as if out of an episode of *Sherlock Holmes Goes to California*.

After that first meeting where I was introduced to the faces of countless people now being forced to fight for the very homes they had fairly purchased from banks, I was struck by the complexity of the message at hand. My friend had grown up in that house. Her parents still lived there. It was an important message, but eminent domain is a complicated idea. I understood, however, that the message needed to be simplified. These people needed to save their homes, and the clarity and simplicity of that idea needed to find a better presentation.

The next month a rally was held. A battle cry rose up, "Hell no, we won't go!" as masses of people crowded downtown to hear the staid voices of an alarmed group of homeowners and politicians. No one was ready to panic, but their voices had to be heard.

"Hell no, we won't go!" came the reverent *amen* from those gathered.

Three months later, a march was held, again with signs and resolute chanting: "Hell no, we won't go!"

The message was correct. The rhythmic center attached itself to the heart of the matter at hand. But the truth was that it wasn't *the* message. It was an old message. It was a beleaguered message that wasn't actually saying anything at all, because it had become clichéd in its overuse; it had become muddled by years of overlapping applications.

At a later meeting at a bar I attended, I learned about an upcoming concert that would feature an illustrious group of celebrities who would amass and turn this small-but-growing gathering into a movement. I understood one thing no one else seemed to see: It needed a mantra; it needed a name, and that name had to be chant-able, bite-sized and arresting in its power.

I went home that day on a personal mission: I pounded out the sound of the words I wanted to hear. Hell no, we won't go. The truth was, we would go if they made us. So I altered the words:

"We will go for the right reasons."

"You should do this right," I tried, putting the onus on them instead of us.

"Build thoughtfully," I considered.

"Build us up," I added, making them responsible to the people.

"Don't ruin our city!" I accused.

"Don't tear us down," I admonished.

I stopped. "Build us up." I said it out loud. "Don't tear us down."

I pounded the rhythm out on the table. "Build. Us. Up. Don't. Tear. Us. Down."

That was it. But it wasn't a title. It was a mantra. "Build Thoughtfully." That felt more like a title. But it didn't feel as much like a mantra. What this corporation planned to do felt to those of us gathered at meetings like a destruction of the city. I continued to hammer it out until finally, I felt like I had it: Progress, Not Conquest.

When I arrived that day at the event, I had made tank tops and tee-shirts with my title/mantra in bold print. I planned to charge face value, which was $7.45 or $8.00 for simplicity's sake. After an hour, all three hundred had been sold and were being worn by many in the crowd. I received two hundred additional orders including several from neighborhood boutiques. I had succeeded.

I spent the next year building a small business with "Progress, Not Conquest." While eventually eminent domain won out and my phrase came to exist as part of the history of my neighborhood, it taught me a lot about business and the value of words.

For me, law school is the logical next step in my life. "Progress, Not Conquest" is something I continue to believe in and hope to live my life fighting for. I promise to do so with language that is concise, rhythmic and powerful.

JDMISSION REVIEW

Overall Lesson

Reflection does not make you a narcissist.

First Impression

The candidate loses me a little when she disparages Chaucer and James Joyce in her second sentence because, well, they are Chaucer and Joyce. I know they are brilliant writers, whereas I do not know her at all—yet.

Strengths

The story she tells is great. It lends itself well to a personal statement in that it demonstrates the candidate's interest in law and the reasons she got involved in the situation she describes. Also, she does not seem to imply that she already knows everything she needs to about how the law works—a mistake many law school applicants tend to make in their personal statement when they bring up a legal concept like eminent domain. Instead, she describes her involvement in a legal issue in a way that is cerebral without trying too hard to sound like a lawyer. The essay is well done, in that sense.

I also really like her phrasing in certain places, such as, "it had become muddled by years of overlapping applications." That kind of wording reveals a writer's sensibility that will carry her far both in law school and in a legal career. Although using specific sequences of words may *seem* trivial, doing so can reveal a great deal about one's propensity to excel as a lawyer because—as you may have heard before—lawyers *write* almost as much as they read.

Weaknesses

When the candidate states, "But it taught me a lot about business and the value of words" at the conclusion of her story, I do not understand what she means.

I imagine she was disappointed with the outcome of the eminent domain challenge. I imagine she wanted to do more than she reasonably could have. But these are my assumptions—I do not know the truth about how she felt or what her real, nuanced take-aways from the situation were. This is an area that applicants neglect all too often in their personal statements, especially in their early drafts. They tell a story and share whether they succeeded or failed, but they do not then reflect on and discuss what it all meant, either then or now, as they are applying to law school.

I understand why—reflection of that kind is hard. It can often be deeply personal, and people do not generally want to tap into certain intense emotions if they do not have to. The inclination is to think that this level of introspection is not necessary for a personal statement. In other words, candidates think, "What does the admissions committee care about how I felt after my mom's death/that pivotal baseball game/the legal case that changed everything?"

However, this is not an anecdote you are simply sharing with family or friends around the dinner table or in a bar. The admissions officers reading your essay really *do* care, because they are interested in understanding how you think, and catering to that interest does not make you narcissistic or boring. The trick is to write down all your heartfelt, sincere reactions to the event you are describing in your essay—and then enlist someone's help in editing it.

Final Assessment

I would encourage the applicant to bolster the part of the essay in which she reacts to the results of the campaign, disappointing as they were. This is the crux of her decision to go to law school, after all. It is therefore a huge part of her story. We need to know more about why she took the campaign and its outcome so much to heart. She also needs to explain how she wants to use the experience to inform her future as a law student and as a lawyer.

PERSONAL STATEMENT 2

Start strong by being clear.

Growing up as the only girl with three older brothers, I developed a strong sense of independence and femininity at a young age. My close relationship with my mother provided sensitivity and comfort, while my brothers and father provided toughness. I have always considered myself a feminist, and my experiences have reinforced that conviction. Throughout my life, I have tried to find the most effective way for me to put my convictions and beliefs into practice. My first thought was politics. In my sophomore year of high school, I founded a political forum, where my classmates met to discuss the most controversial political issues, and everyone was invited to share her point of view. The topic that always brought out the strongest reaction in me was violence against women and the sexual oppression of women – subjects that, in my opinion, do not receive enough attention or outrage. Issues such as child marriage, forced prostitution, and sex-selective abortion are just a few that come to mind.

At Davidson College, I developed a strong interest in the history of women in Middle Eastern and Asian countries. I chose to focus on the suffering of women in these regions, exploring in particular the historical roots of certain heinous practices, such as "honor killings," bride burning (dowry deaths), *sati* (widow burning), and female genital mutilation. I wrote my senior thesis about the history of *sati*, an ancient Indian practice in which a widow throws herself on her husband's funeral pyre and burns alive with his corpse. Although the practice was outlawed by the British in 1829, it continued on thereafter and even occurs today, although it is rare.

I decided to study abroad in order to witness firsthand what it was like to be a woman in a developing country. For four months during my junior year of college, I traveled around India with ten classmates. My expectations prior to my trip were mixed. On one hand, India has tremendous natural beauty and a rich history. On the other hand, India has a culture that so undervalues girls that there are 914 female children for every 1,000 male children according to India's 2011 census. Compare that to nearby Thailand, where the male to female sex ratio is a much more even 0.98. While visiting the Indian state of Karnataka, I learned about the *devadasi* system, which forces unwanted girls into a life of sex work in the name of Hinduism. Although the system was outlawed in 1988, it is still very much in existence. While visiting the Visthar organization in Bangalore, I met a widow who explained to me the horrible treatment and isolation she experienced in society upon the death of her husband. She was no longer allowed to in any way ornament herself, forced to wear a plain white sheet for the rest of her life. Her many bangles were ceremoniously shattered against a rock, a symbolic gesture. I learned about how many young women die in seeming "accidents," often involving stoves, when their in-laws think their dowry is insufficient.

My experience was not limited to observation. I had some disturbing moments myself as a young woman traveling in India. While visiting the National Museum of Delhi, a major tourist attraction, a group of several young school boys on a field trip surrounded and attacked me, and no one seemed to care, even though I cried for help. No one helped me. No police officers. No teachers. No one. Luckily I was able to break through and get away. I knew that things could have been much worse: rape is a huge problem in India. There are horrific stories of girls being gang-raped in public. Often the police do not even bother to search for the perpetrators, and sometimes the rape victim is blamed for "inviting" the attack. These episodes are extremely disturbing, and they are not limited to this one country.

Unfortunately, many cultures throughout the world continue to treat women like second-class citizens. I have resolved to make it my life's work to stop violent crimes against women. I may not be able to affect whole cultures in my lifetime, but as a lawyer I can help women who have been wronged. In addition, I can make it my mission to prosecute those who mistreat women to the full extent of the law. That is what I plan to do with my law degree, to be a servant of Justice, for women in America and hopefully all over the world.

JDMISSION REVIEW

Overall Lesson

Start strong by starting clearly.

First Impression

The first few sentences of this essay seem to be pulling in different directions—the writing is fine, but the focus is unclear. Is she going to talk about her family? Her feminism? Her political interests? If these topics were all clearly related, this would not be an issue, but I do not readily see the connection. Consider how each of these three sentences—three of her first four—read as topic sentences: "Growing up as the only girl with three older brothers, I developed a strong sense of independence and femininity at a young age." "I have always considered myself a feminist, and my experiences have reinforced that conviction." "Throughout my life, I have tried to find the most effective way for me to put my convictions and beliefs into practice." Any of these could be the topic of her first paragraph, but not all three of them.

Strengths

The applicant offers details that are unequivocally hers, deeply personal, and in fact, somewhat alarming: "While visiting the National Museum of Delhi, a major tourist attraction, a group of several young school boys on a field trip surrounded and attacked me, and no one seemed to care, even though I cried for help. No one helped me. No police officers. No teachers. No one." What is compelling about this is that she is not trying to terrify us as readers, but her frankness in listing those who ignored her cries allows us to empathize with her experience and understand how it led to the passion she claims to feel for gender issues now.

Weaknesses

The applicant tells us in the first paragraph that she learned sensitivity from her mother and toughness from her father and brothers. Since she does not then explicitly link these qualities to feminism, however, the connection is unclear. (Indeed, some might say that "feminism" is not reflected in such expected gendered descriptions at all.) Because "feminism" is a term that has evolved over numerous phases of cultural change and could therefore refer to a wide range of ideas—some of which conflict—being clearer about precisely what she means here would be good.

She could also create a more compelling picture of her emergence as an independent thinker by adding more specific details to her first paragraph. Suppose her first sentence read (we are making this up), "Growing up as the only girl among three football-playing older brothers, I vacillated between being protected, being ignored and being ridiculed. This ping-ponging around traditional female roles shaped how I viewed the world." In this example, tangible details plus a higher level of analysis make the story fully hers, meaning it could not belong to just anyone with a one-sister, three-brother upbringing. It also reveals her ability to step back from a situation and analyze its dynamic.

Although the chronological structure of the essay works, the applicant's story could have been presented another way equally effectively. She does not need to start with her family dynamic or childhood. What if she had begun with a more mature version of herself—such as how she chose to make a study of *sati* the topic of her major?

Final Assessment

Overall, this candidate has conveyed that she is applying to law school with a sense of personal purpose. Her commitment to defending women's rights comes across as sincere and informed. She could still improve on her execution of this idea, particularly at the beginning, but the final two-thirds make up for the slightly disjointed and overly general start.

PERSONAL STATEMENT 3

Make your ending as strong
as your beginning.

In the aftermath of the Parker City tornado in the spring of 2008, an urgent call went out at 3PM from a first aid station in that beleaguered town to Grandview Hospital in Des Moines, where I was working as an EMT. A physician's presence was desperately needed that very afternoon. I was not a physician, but I had been extensively trained in emergency medical care. If no one else could heed the call, I knew I would take it.

My shift was ending. So I radioed that I was heading down. After threading my way through several roadblocks, I finally arrived at what I now saw was a standing elementary school converted into a "first aid station" in the middle of a jumble of fallen buildings. Children's gym mats were doubling as beds, with upwards of thirty people with minor but painful injuries seeking help.

By this time, the more gravely injured patients had been transported to larger nearby hospitals. Seventy people had been reported missing or dead, which in a population of 1,500 is enough to leave a mark.

I did what I could to help the patients, cleaning and taping wounds, splinting sprains, and diagnosing more serious breaks in order to send those individuals along to the hospital. Around 3AM a young woman came in. Her water had broken, and she was clearly in labor. She told me she was three weeks early. Her contractions were close enough together that it was clear to me she probably wouldn't make it the fifty minutes to the hospital. We called for an OB and were told one would make it in an hour. In the meantime, I prepared to deliver the baby.

It would be my second emergency delivery and fourth assist. I felt confident in my abilities and understood exactly what was expected of me. I was certain to explain this to the young lady to help lessen her panic. She called me "doctor." I opted not to correct her.

During an emergency, it is important as an aide worker to help legitimate emergency stations. The minute the population in need begins to doubt our efficacy, our purpose becomes immediately obsolete. Upon my arrival to the station, although the environment was visibly subdued, a palpable sense of relief spread from makeshift-bed to makeshift-bed, almost immediately. My arrival legitimated this first aide station. As a medical aide worker, although I am not an M.D. or D.O., I chose to act as one.

Of course, I never called myself doctor, and more than once made the correction. "I am an EMT," telling patients and co-workers alike. But as the only medic on hand, I lent an air of authority that the outlet desperately required to complete the mission at hand.

I delivered a baby girl that morning. She was healthy despite her early arrival. When the OB arrived ten minutes after her birth, he was able to confirm the bright health of the mother and baby. We shook hands. He stayed for another hour and then left them in my care.

I expected eventually to hear from the young mother regarding the birth of her child. I thought perhaps I would be lucky enough to get a picture and a thank you. Instead I received a summons. I was being sued. I was accused of misrepresenting myself. She was stating that she would have made the fifty-minute drive to the hospital had she known I was not a "real" doctor. The truth was, yes, she might have made it to deliver her girl, although just barely. The baby girl was healthy, but the young mother felt that the normal developmental delays for a baby born three weeks early could have been avoided if she'd driven to the hospital.

I had the support of the staff of the "first aid station" (which she was also attempting to sue). My lawyer told me not to testify, but staff members and other co-workers spoke on my behalf of my loyalty, honesty and sense of duty. The whole experience was a humbling one to say the least. And in the end, we won. But I had become gun shy, and it made me wonder if perhaps I had reached the end of that road. That feeling grew with time until finally, like my military career before it, I felt that I was ready for something new.

Simultaneously completing my undergrad degree, I decided that law school was the next logical place for me. I actually feel like my military background and experience as an EMT compliment a career in law in a way few other skill-sets ever could. My experience is in bringing a sense of security to emergency situations. Imagine what I could do in an environment that is deliberate and thoughtful, like the law.

JdMISSION REVIEW

Overall Lesson

Do not write an impassioned essay with a tepid ending.

First Impression

The first paragraph is great. I am drawn into the scene, and the stakes are high. I understand the applicant's predicament. In just a few words, he conveys his willingness to go beyond the call of duty: "If no one else could heed the call, I knew I would take it."

Strengths

Although being sued is awful, this significant event in the candidate's life was an ideal subject choice for his personal statement. He effectively tells the story, too—it is gripping, and although I am rooting for him, I also understand the concerns of the plaintiff/mother who sued him. A true sign of effective writing is when you are able to empathize with parties on both sides of a dispute.

Weaknesses

The candidate has me right up until the end, when his energy fizzles. Contrast the powerful beginning with the essay's last two sentences: "My experience is in bringing a sense of security to emergency situations. Imagine what I could do in an environment that is deliberate and thoughtful, like the law."

Why is the applicant asking the reader to imagine his potential? He should be explicit here. What does he believe he could accomplish or contribute in a legal environment? What does he want to do within the legal realm? He should explain why being sued did more than humble him, how it also made him want to pursue law. This essay's ending needs to be significantly more robust to make the piece work as part of a law school application.

Allow me to make another important point:

> *Compliment* = to make a formal expression of esteem, respect, affection, or admiration

> *Complement* = to fill in or make up what is lacking, to supplement

Do not confuse the two in your essay, because the admissions committee will notice your mistake.

Final Assessment

This essay needs substantial work in the final two paragraphs; they do not convey the same sense of confidence, urgency, or level of detail as the others. I would advise this applicant to revise them until they are as convincing and compelling as the paragraphs that make up the first two-thirds of the essay.

PERSONAL STATEMENT 4

Remember your goal.

When my wife died at forty of Huntington's disease, it was not a surprise. Long before we lived in our suburban New Jersey home and raised our three children, long before I met her serving me a lemonade at the café frequented by NYU undergrads, she had been told that someday this would be how her life would end.

She told me on our fourth date about her fate to die young, but I already knew at that point that I wanted to be around her for as long as I could be. We got married on a Sunday in the backyard of her mother's home. We danced until everyone went home, stayed up until the sun came up. I graduated from NYU with a degree in education. We adopted our three children and I worked for twenty-five years as a high school math teacher at the private school where we sent our kids.

After my wife's excruciating convalescence and subsequent death, I made a decision not to go back to work. Our kids did the best they could to finish out their college careers. My oldest got married. I walked her down the aisle at her beautiful wedding and tried not to cry at the sight of the stunning woman her mother would never get to see.

When one year later my daughter gave birth to our grandchild and gave her my wife's name, I tried to anticipate their needs like her mother would have, to disappointing results, I am certain. My life was a quiet one. When my daughter and her two year old showed up asking to spend the night, I was happy to have them. When my daughter's marriage dissolved and she asked if they could stay indefinitely, I felt grateful. Having my granddaughter in the house was a joy. I enjoyed having the little-girl laughter back under my roof.

I thought of us as a team. She helped to keep up the house and I babysat and spent time with them. She prodded me to go back to my job. But that route felt wrong. I wanted to do something bigger with my life than teach numbers. So I began looking into life in politics. I had always wanted to go to law school, but my wife and I had wanted to start our family. I suddenly saw the possibility. The death of my wife and the birth of my beloved granddaughter had meaning that I was only just beginning to understand. I began to refocus my goals.

I hate to admit it was children's music that finally pushed me to register for the LSAT, but when my now-four-year-old granddaughter played the same Disney movie for the umpteenth time, I made my move. Staying home was no longer the right thing for me.

My daughter and my granddaughter tell they are proud of me. My younger children have told me that I am making the decision they'd been hoping I would. In fact, my youngest and I are filling out our graduate school applications together. He intends to go into Engineering, a choice of which his mother would be endlessly proud.

I look at the success of our family, and I know my wife would want me to make this choice and move in this direction. I feel like I have her love and support with every step I take. I only hope I can achieve my dreams without her by my side.

jdMission Review

Overall Lesson

Although your essay may be 90% of the way to where it needs to be, that last 10% may be the most important.

First Impression

Oh, my. His story is crushing. After the first paragraph, I am hooked—now, the candidate needs to maintain the strength of his essay.

Strengths

I find the candidate extremely engaging as a writer and as a person, though his story is, of course, difficult to read. The premature death of a life partner is traumatic, and the pain of his experience is manifest in the details. But even though I found his story sadly compelling, and I sympathize with him and am rooting for him, his essay does not persuade me that he should be in law school.

Weaknesses

I want the candidate to succeed, but that is because he is endearing and I admire him as a person—*not* because he has successfully convinced me that both he and the school would benefit from his admission.

Fortunately for him, solving this problem should not be too difficult. He could cut some details about his history with his wife (how they met, perhaps) as well as about his daughter and granddaughter moving in with him. This would free up space that he could instead devote to discussing why he wants to get his JD, rather than just mentioning that he "began looking into life in politics" and earlier in life had "always wanted to go to law school."

Why does he want to go now, besides his desire to get back in the saddle, so to speak? What are his legal interests? How does he envision his future career in law?

Final Assessment

This candidate is starting over—good for him! But his essay needs to do more than just announce that he is starting over. It needs discuss in greater detail why he has chosen law school as his particular means of doing so.

PERSONAL STATEMENT 5

Know your audience.

Cosplay, short for "costume play" saved my life. It is very like performance art, whereby the players generally hand-make costumes that represent popular or iconic characters. Some people go a step beyond simply "wearing" the costumes, and actually role-play the character. For me cosplay was never about fandom. I didn't play a single character over and over. Instead, I played multiple characters, sometimes at the same event. It was about creating the costume and the character and then embodying that role. My sources varied and included anime, manga, literary figures, characters from TV, comic books, video games and film. Sometimes the characters weren't female (crossplaying), and sometimes they weren't even human. Other times altogether, they were entirely inanimate.

The most memorable types of cosplay have a sexual component. Admittedly, most of my costumes involved bikini-wear and minimal fabric. This is true, because many of my favorite characters are best represented by their beautiful and sexual bodies, but also because I enjoyed the attention these outfits afforded me. However, I only ever embodied strong female archetypes. My cosplay was decidedly feminist.

I believe it is common to consider cosplay a hobby, but for me it was an identity born out of multiple identities – each of which brought me a little bit closer to myself. Before cosplay I was "Joan Smythe," nerd and loner. In high school I was so out of touch with who I was, I literally wore my brother's clothes and agreed with them when my fellow students called me a "dyke" or a "loser." I discovered cosplay my senior year, and when I did, nothing my classmates called me mattered, because that girl in the oversized t-shirt and cargo pants wasn't the same girl wearing the Queen Amidala wig and white battle costume that she'd made herself.

It wasn't a Halloween stunt, as my mother suggested, or a childish pastime, as my father believed. It was an identity that made me stronger, smarter and more creative than I'd ever been as Joan. So I changed my name to Jane, the cosplayer, the costume designer, the role-player, and I grew within that woman to become someone strong and capable. In the places where I met with other cosplayers, I belonged.

For me, as important as the events and competitions are themselves, it is the photo shoots I meticulously stage with every costume that outshine everything else. I am lucky enough to consistently work with thoughtful photographers who are willing to work with me until we achieve my vision. I apply my make up with an eye toward the photographs over the events, using thick coats and brush strokes to achieve maximum theatricality.

Copsplay is no longer my escape. It is my reality. The idea of entering a fantasy world, counterintuitive though it may seem, can actually serve as a guidepost toward the certainty of a soul. I know myself better and in more detail than I did when I was younger. Of course, one might say, the same is true of making friends. Creating a circle of intimate friends and close acquaintances provides living mirrors through which one might best understand oneself. Before cosplay, I didn't have any of these.

It is clear to me that cosplay is a tool by which I have come to know myself. Overtime I have come to take it less seriously and embrace it as an outlet of entertainment. But the woman that has developed within it is one that knows her goals and understands her own mind. I will always cosplay, but that will only be a portion of who I am. I believe that a law school education is exactly the evolution the character, "Jane Smith" needs to achieve. But I also believe that a great law school program such as the one you offer, will similarly evolve for the better with my acceptance into your program. You will be gaining a creative, confident and self-aware woman for whom stepping out of her own skin and into someone else's only serves to make her more herself.

Thank you.

JdMission Review

Overall Lesson

Know your audience.

First Impression

At the end of the first paragraph, I still do not know what "cosplay" is. Is this happening in a park? Is it something that goes on through all of life? What is the "play" component—is it just dressing up in costumes, or does it involve an activity? She could be much clearer about the answers to these questions.

Strengths

This applicant is a decent writer and understands that the fundamental goal of the personal statement is to convey that she is a person the admissions committee wants at its school. I know this because of how she ends: "You will be gaining a creative, confident and self-aware woman for whom stepping out of her own skin and into someone else's only serves to make her more herself."

Weaknesses

Despite her understanding of the purpose of a personal statement, she misses the mark with regard to execution. Using one's personal statement to discuss how one's hobbies have led to one's self-realization is fine, and if those hobbies are unusual, that is fine as well. But what is not fine is if a hobby comes across as a tool for handling a psychological issue that could impede one's ability to be a lawyer. And unfortunately, that is how "cosplay" sounds in this essay.

In addition to not even really understanding what cosplay *is*—it appears to involve her dressing up and just existing in various personas—I do not know what the take-away from it is for her as an adult, only what the activity meant to her in high school, when she was lonely and nerdy. That is fine. Talk about that. But then the following sentence suggests that in the present day, she continues to dress as multiple personas: "Copsplay is no longer my escape. It is my reality. The idea of entering a fantasy world, counterintuitive though it may seem, can actually serve as a guidepost toward the certainty of a soul."

This does not make her sound like someone who will make a good lawyer.

I also want to address this sentence: "The most memorable types of cosplay have a sexual component. Admittedly, most of my costumes involved bikini-wear and minimal fabric."

I know that law school, and the legal profession, are viewed by many—including me—as excessively traditional. But that is because these institutions *are* excessively traditional, and the point of the personal statement is to be *admitted* to this excessively traditional world. I could not in good conscience advise a candidate to write about being a sexual hobbyist, especially without contextualizing such a remark better than she does. For example, she calls it "decidedly feminist," but she does not explain how or why or what feminism means to her. A comment like this must read as a necessary piece of information to her story, and the story itself should read as critical to who she is and what she wants to do in law.

When I reach the point of the essay at which this sentence appears, I am confused as to why she is sharing this information, and—if I am putting on my admissions-officer-with-who-knows-what-values-and-beliefs hat—I am dubious about her choice to include it, maybe even dubious about her suitability for a law career, based on her decision to share the information with an admissions committee.

Lawyers are fired all the time for showing up scantily clothed to events or for appearing scantily clad in photos on social media sites. Hate that reality if you want, but if this is a battle you want to fight, fight it *after* you secure a law job;

do not sabotage your legal career before it even starts by including gratuitous personal information in your application.

Final Assessment

I would want to have a frank conversation with this applicant about what the legal profession is like and how she expects to exist within it. I am not implying that she should not attend law school, but she needs to understand that living in costumes is not going to work in 99% of the profession, and suggesting, even implicitly, that that is what she believes is certainly not going to help her get accepted to her target JD program. She may still be able to incorporate the subject of cosplay into an appropriate story about herself, one that *would* lend itself to law school admittance, but this story has a long way to go before it is ready to be submitted to any school.

Personal Statement 6

Provide evidence to support your claims.

Since my route to applying for law school has been somewhat circuitous, I feel it is relevant to describe the guiding principles that have determined my trajectory. I freely admit that this decision does not represent the culmination of a lifelong dream—a point that, for me, is evidence that I have made the right choice. In short, these principles are a committed passion for learning "why the world wags and what wags it" (Merlyn's description of learning in T.H. White's *The Once and Future King* [1958]) and a genuine concern for the environment. These two strands, having each grown stronger as I have matured, have come together to help me clarify my values, and therefore my interests and goals.

While intellectual curiosity often wanes after college, I have experienced the opposite inclination. Upon graduating in 2005, I resisted the temptation to take what seemed like the next logical step: the pursuit of a graduate degree in literature, my undergraduate field of study. Instead, I accepted a position as a college admissions counselor at my alma mater, and in my free time, read prodigiously and thought honestly about continuing my formal education. I took a class in environmental science, audited two in philosophy, and did everything I could to become not only more informed, but more thoughtful. Since then, I have expanded my realm of awareness and interest to the point that I find nearly everything—from literature to science to politics—an opportunity for intellectual engagement. While this attribute has its downfalls—a single person cannot learn the world in a lifetime—I feel fortunate to have had this passion instilled in me from a young age, even if it has only truly begun to flourish in the past several years.

Having worked full-time for two years, I applied and was accepted on full fellowship to the master's program in Environmental Philosophy at the University of North Texas (a leading program in the field). The impetus behind my decision was a desire to develop a meaningful framework in which to situate my concern for the environment. Today, issues such as sustainable energy and development, the imminent threats posed by global climate change, and the accelerating, anthropogenic loss of biodiversity occupy a central role in the media and public discourse. Despite the increasing recognition of the importance and even urgency of these issues, there continues to be a dearth of agreed-upon, concrete policies to address them. In addition to the obstacle of the detrimental economic impacts of scaling back our resource consumption, there is the fervently debated question of who should be held responsible and how. Furthermore, there is a plethora of arguments as to why these problems must be addressed: among others, ensuring a livable planet for future generations, conserving endangered species, protecting people in vulnerable parts of the world, and providing for the continued flourishing of human civilization. The question of what constitutes the core of our obligation to the natural environment is at the heart of environmental ethics, and it has brought many of my concerns into sharp focus.

At this point, I became interested in the relevance of these questions to policy and lawmaking. The "linear model" of science-based policy (i.e., the more scientific data we accumulate, the easier it will be to make effective decisions) is incomplete. Gains in scientific understanding and technology must be complemented by meaningful discourse about our environmental values. Otherwise, we (at the individual, national, and international levels) may never adequately address these problems that, in terms of both physical and temporal scales, represent uncharted territory. We would be better equipped to more effectively (and democratically) address environmental problems if there were mechanisms in place for candidly discussing and incorporating values into our decision-making, with the understanding that doing so is neither "biased" nor "unscientific," but a legitimate and indispensable component of the process.

My interest in this juncture of ethical thought and practical implementation led me to consider environmental law. I emphasize "led me," because, on its own, such an academic interest is insufficient to warrant attending law school and entering the profession; for example, one could easily explore these questions within academia. But while I hope to have the opportunity to inform my work with theory, my personality and goals are more aligned with praxis. Within environmental law, I can envision myself working in a variety of capacities in both the non-profit and government sectors. However, I will not be in a position to make an informed decision in that regard until I have actually attended law school; any thoughts on such specific career goals are merely speculative.

As I began to research and think through the possibility of pursuing a law career, I found myself becoming increasingly interested in studying and practicing law more generally. While my concern for the environment was the entry point for considering law school, it came to serve as a catalyst to open my eyes to a broader interest in the law. Therefore, I wish to make it abundantly clear that I plan to attend with a consciously open mind, harking back to the overarching principle of intellectual pursuit that guides me. Since it is likely unsurprising that New York University is my first choice, given my interests, I will not elaborate excessively on that point. While I reiterate that I am approaching law school with an open mind, I do know that I want to work for the public interest in some capacity; hence, I am attracted to NYU's unparalleled commitment to and opportunities in public interest law. My interest in environmental law would be fulfilled by the myriad opportunities within the program (including the presence on the faculty of Affiliate Professor Dale Jamieson, whose work I know from his contributions to environmental philosophy). Having done extensive research on NYU's curriculum, centers, faculty, and clinical opportunities, I cannot imagine a better fit for me. Having given myself the time and life experience necessary to make a thoughtful and meaningful decision, I am confident that my values and interests are eminently consistent with this career choice. I genuinely look forward to beginning my law studies, and hope, in turn, to bring valuable perspectives and experience to the table. Thank you for your consideration.

jdMission Review

Overall Lesson

If you claim that you care about something, prove it by offering substantive evidence.

First Impression

This essay begins in a similar fashion to another one in this book, but it succeeds where that one fails. For comparison, let us examine the introductory paragraphs from both essays. The other essay begins as follows:

> It may come as a surprise to anyone reading this that someone like myself thinks I have a shot at going to a law school as prestigious as [the target school]. However, it is exactly people like me who I think would make the best lawyers. I have had to struggle my whole life to learn what it is I want to do—be a lawyer—and thus come to the practice with a greater sense of purpose than many people I know who have wanted to be lawyers ever since seeing their first *Law and Order* episode.

This essay begins with the following:

> Since my route to applying for law school has been somewhat circuitous, I feel it is relevant to describe the guiding principles that have determined my trajectory. I freely admit that this decision does not represent the culmination of a lifelong dream—a point that, for me, is evidence that I have made the right choice. In short, these principles are a committed passion for learning "why the world wags and what wags it" and a genuine concern for the environment. These two strands, having each grown stronger as I have matured, have

come together to help me clarify my values, and therefore my interests and goals.

These introductory paragraphs are notably different. Although both candidates emphasize that they have not been aspiring to become lawyers since they were children, the former does so in a sloppy, somewhat apologetic way, while the latter is confident, clear, and poised in her explanation.

Strengths

The candidate's essay unfolds in a way that works structurally. She introduces how she was led to law, goes on to describe her path in more detail, and ends with her vision for her legal education and career.

But she also accomplishes two specific goals. First, in the third paragraph, she does something far too few candidates do, and even fewer do well: she actually describes the issues she claims to care about. She could have stopped at "The impetus behind my decision was a desire to develop a meaningful framework in which to situate my concern for the environment." Instead, she goes on to describe *in precise terms* what she means: "sustainable energy and development, the imminent threats posed by global climate change, and the accelerating, anthropogenic loss of biodiversity."

Second, she delves deeper into what she believes makes these issues so urgent: "there continues to be a dearth of agreed-upon, concrete policies to address them." And although she might have ended her argument there, she continues, reiterating her sincere, thoughtful passion for the environment: "Furthermore, there is a plethora of arguments as to why these problems must be addressed: among others, ensuring a livable planet for future generations, conserving endangered species, protecting people in vulnerable parts of the world, and providing for the continued flourishing of human civilization."

By the end of the third paragraph, I am persuaded of her concern for the environment; she has actually proven it by naming the issues, identifying the problems that arise in addressing them, and noting the stakes.

Weaknesses

Despite being well written, her penultimate paragraph is superfluous and errs on the side of apologizing for or overexplaining her interest in law school, which candidates should never do. All but the first line of it should be eliminated. I would advise her to cut text as shown here, and then make the first sentence of what is currently the last paragraph the second sentence of this paragraph:

> My interest in this juncture of ethical thought and practical implementation led me to consider environmental law. ~~I emphasize "led me," because, on its own, such an academic interest is insufficient to warrant attending law school and entering the profession; for example, one could easily explore these questions within academia. But while I hope to have the opportunity to inform my work with theory, my personality and goals are more aligned with praxis. Within environmental law, I can envision myself working in a variety of capacities in both the non-profit and government sectors. However, I will not be in a position to make an informed decision in that regard until I have actually attended law school; any thoughts on such specific career goals are merely speculative.~~ As I began to research and think through the possibility of pursuing a law career, I found myself becoming increasingly interested in studying and practicing law more generally.

Finally, the candidate rambles a bit in the last paragraph when assuring the school that she is not interested *only* in environmental law. I did not think her interest was limited to that field, so in my case, at least, she is trying to disprove an assumption that I had not actually made.

In addition—and this is a minor point—the sentence "While this attribute has its downfalls—a single person cannot learn the world in a lifetime—I feel fortunate to have had this passion instilled in me" does not really make sense. The inability to "learn the world in a lifetime" is not a downfall but a fact; no one can do this. She should either describe an actual downfall (e.g., "I am constantly frustrated," "I can never become an expert in any one thing, which is irritating") or express the idea differently.

Final Assessment

I would encourage this candidate to streamline her final paragraph and advise her to cut some of the text as I explained earlier in this review. However, I would also compliment her on writing a strong essay and wish her the best of luck in what will surely be a successful and satisfying career in law.

PERSONAL STATEMENT 7

Clearly connect the dots.

Tutweiler, Mississippi, 2004

A warm breeze heralded the arrival of another ghostly Delta night as I studied the back wall of the abandoned train depot. Facing me was a grotesque mural depicting a sinister bluesman and a crude map to his grave. The story of a harmonica player, the famed Aleck "Rice" Miller, had drawn me to this forgotten fold in America's cultural fabric. As I searched for answers in the smears of color clinging to the worn bricks, I could not help but wonder what had made me so receptive to Miller's pull.

More than a year after my Delta pilgrimage, hindsight has given me a better understanding of my obsession with the blues. I now have a better understanding of my fascination with all of the seemingly unrelated activities that dot my history. After a short lifetime spent skating in circles as fast as possible, I suddenly redirected my efforts along an academic bead. Now, with my undergraduate career behind me, the law has captured my attention. As puzzling as these choices have been to me and to others, my relationship with structure connects the dots of these disparate interests. Structure is a point of reference, a context that gives information relevance. It is how I see structure built into my pursuits that makes sense of my life.

I relished speed skating's repetition. I have skated thousands of miles in four hundred meter units, each lap an opportunity to improve upon the last. It is a game of uniformity—the same track, the same distance, and the same physics that bind every athlete—yet no two skaters reach the finish line the same way. I admired the best competitors for their ability to internalize the rules of the sport and creatively discover ways to find speed within these boundaries. The knowledge that I was milking physics for every drop of speed made the apex of a turn—the point at which a skater most acutely feels the constraints of Newton's laws—even more exhilarating.

I see the blues in a similar light. Renowned for its raw, unbridled creativity, the blues is a highly structured genre; most blues records utilize just three chords arranged into a strict and repetitive harmonic formula. Ironically, the creative potency of the blues finds its roots in this rigidity. The harmonic changes of a blues progression, through endless repetition, create expectations in the listener's ear. A true master recognizes potential energy in these expectations. The best soloists use the music's structure as a point of reference and build meaning in relation to it. It is this context that gives a simple harmonica lick the power to pull its listeners through the entire emotional spectrum, from the most desperate, empty lows to the most jubilant, elated highs.

Presently working for the Antitrust Division of the U. S. Department of Justice, I am beginning to see the law the same way. Two weeks into my employment, I witnessed a dynamic argument between two attorneys shouldering different philosophies of antitrust law. The attorneys' intellects soared as they endeavored to find novel ways to understand the legal situation at hand. Yet structure anchored the discussion; by providing context, the law made the attorneys' ideas appreciable. I recognized their impressive creativity in relation to the stable framework of the law. Though the law and its intricacies are still very much a mystery to me, I am slowly excavating the structure that girds them.

Structure reveals who I am; it is a glimpse of my own personal blueprint. I access the ideas, events, and people around me by recognizing frameworks. Once I connect to my surroundings, my actual approach also integrates structure. I love to spot the rules of a system and navigate through them, discovering what I can create in the process. It is this type of creativity—creativity within context—that truly inspires me. My major interests may not be inherently connected. But the way I perceive them and the way I approach their challenges is the same.

JDMISSION REVIEW

Overall Lesson

Do not write a beautiful essay that implies you do not belong in law school.

First Impression

The candidate's first paragraph is unusual and enchanting, the writing strong and mysterious. I am curious about where the essay is going, but I certainly do not have my footing yet.

Strengths

As associate dean of admissions at Yale Law School, Asha Rangappa wrote about personal statements on the school's admissions blog [bolding added]:

> The great personal statement makes connections between the experiences or events that the applicant has highlighted and, say, a larger idea or theme that it made the applicant consider or explore further. Or, for someone who wrote about their upbringing or background, perhaps **they now evaluate those experiences from a new and different perspective and can make a connection between those experiences and issues they later became interested in.** Another way to put this is that this type of personal statement takes something that was merely *descriptive*—a cover letter—and makes it into something that is *reflective*—an essay.

This essay strikes me as a good example of what Rangappa describes. The candidate introduces himself by discussing his interest in the blues style of music. He then reflects on where that interest originated and effectively connects the origin to his other life interests—speed skating and law—which on the surface do not seem related at all.

Weaknesses

Although this essay is extremely well written—cogent, interesting, insightful, reflective—by the end, I find myself thinking, "Wow, good essay. But wait—*why* does he want to go to law school?" By highlighting the "structural" similarities among his three areas of interest, the candidate demonstrates that he is an innovative thinker. However, he does not explain what about law makes him want to study it, apart from the opportunity to reenact this process of discovering creativity through limitations, which is quite poetic. As an admissions officer with a law degree, however, I may wonder how this candidate envisions his legal career. Creativity may be part of it, but much, much more of the profession involves tedium, logical analysis, and reading, reading, reading.

Final Assessment

I would help this candidate flesh out the section of his essay in which he discusses his interest in law. He does not necessarily need to change what he has already written, but he could add a paragraph showing that he understands the nature of a legal career and has chosen it knowing all the facts. With such an addition, I think the candidate could transform his essay from strong to fantastic.

Personal Statement 8

Leave no doubt about your candidacy.

It all began in the bedroom of a fourteen-year-old high school outcast. I had transferred from John Cortes High School, in a big urban center, to Sam Houston High in a completely rural part of the state. There were 58 kids in my class, which felt big, especially when one considered how much space separated each of us in our blips of family farm houses surrounded as they were by eons of crop lines, quiet roads and stray grasses, ponds and trees.

The difference between those other 57 kids and I was simple: Their families were farmers and had been for years. Mine were actors who suddenly decided they wanted to own a farm. At first I felt like Leslie Burke in *Bridge to Terabithia* without my "Jesse Aarons" counterpart. I wore mismatched socks and bright t-shirts. Sometimes I wore two different-color converse sneakers. I thought it was cool. The kids in my class thought it was freakish. They hadn't spent junior high with a Sarah Rapier who wore all black and drew raccoon eyes with her mother's eyeliner and made all the other students call her "Roach," or a Charlie Sugg who was blind and autistic and counted out loud when he didn't mean to.

By the time freshman year ended, I came to associate expansive land with loneliness. So I'd find ways to fill the space. I started on my bedroom window—the one closest to my head as I lay on my bed. I painted straight lines and circles, eventually filling up my line of vision with colorful landscapes that did not include rows of corn. Eventually the entire sheet of glass had been transformed. I followed the first with another, and another until all four windows in my room glowed, colorful screens.

When I started painting the window at the top of the stairs, no one complained. But as it neared completion, my parents suggested I check out a nearby architectural salvage yard and take my work outside. I spent a lot of time at that salvage yard. I was drawn to the older, weathered wooden frames. I began to scrape the frames bare and painted them bright colors, then sell them (or more often, give them away). I wound up in art school.

Sometimes art school takes passion and turns it into something practical. For me, my studies became less "art school" and more liberal arts school. I took classes outside the art building at the university, ones that would prepare me for a career in law, something that I slowly took interest in after several history classes changed my perspective on the world.

I graduated with a dual major in Painting and American History. The next step for me is law school. Painting was a way out of my skin during a time when I felt isolated and alone. It was my salvation, allowing me to imagine worlds where I belonged. College brought me a profound sense of belonging, thanks in large part to my paintings, and let me discover myself. It set me on a path toward law school, and toward me.

JDMISSION REVIEW

Overall Lesson

If you went to a nontraditional college, you will need to do more to show that you are prepared to handle the rigors of law school.

First Impression

Meh. The writing is not great. For example, some sentences are unclear, such as this one: "There were fifty-eight kids in my class, which felt big, especially when one considered how much space separated each of us in our blips of family farm houses surrounded as they were by eons of crop lines, quiet roads and stray grasses, ponds and trees." I also am expecting the candidate to start talking about being a loner at 14, which as far as personal statement topics go, is not especially interesting or insightful.

Strengths

The essay does ultimately cover some interesting ground. I like that the candidate explains what inspired her to paint, and in turn, to attend art school. I also think she smoothly outlines the transition from art to law without sounding as though she is apologizing for not having gone to a liberal arts institution.

Weaknesses

Off the bat, several minor issues need to be addressed:

1. In the sentence "The difference between those other fifty-seven kids and I was simple," the phrase "the other kids and I" should instead read "the other kids and me" to be grammatically correct.

2. The applicant should not assume that her reader is familiar with the movie *Bridge to Terabithia* and can therefore readily understand any references to its

plot or main characters. The intended meaning of her allusion to the story is immediately lost on any reader who does not know the film.

3. In general, speaking for others is a bad idea, so sentences like "The kids in my class thought it was freakish" should be avoided. If the other students actually *called* her a freak or said that how she dressed was freakish, she should say *that*. However, if she is merely interpreting their actions in this way, she should cushion her assumptions in more subjective language—such as, "Around the other kids, however, I felt like a freak."

Still, the most important issue here is that in reviewing her application, the law school admissions committees will definitely question whether art school effectively prepared her for the challenges of law school. She needs to do more to convince the reader that she is equipped to handle a rigorous law school curriculum. Her passion for painting is lovely, and reading about it helps the reader develop a more complete image of her as a person, but the question remains: will she be able to work through hundreds of pages of dense reading each week, then conduct thorough, insightful legal analysis? The essay right now does not persuade me that she will.

Final Assessment

I want the candidate to work on the section in which she discusses her college coursework and what she learned. I particularly would like to hear more about her history classes and American history major. Did she write a thesis? What did she learn about research and writing? What in particular about American history captivated her?

The candidate would also benefit from adding at least a brief discussion of the law-related career she envisions for herself. How exactly does she plan to apply her degree after graduating? We need to know where she believes her "path" will take her next.

PERSONAL STATEMENT 9

Select a topic that will not
overshadow you.

Suddenly, there I was, twenty-three years old and standing in line at CVS with a giant, conspicuous box of adult diapers. When I got to the check out, the pretty blond behind the cash register looked at me quizzically. "For my grandma," I said.

I was one year out of school and working for a preeminent law firm as a paralegal, when something began going terribly wrong. Earlier that day I had been in a meeting with a partner when the urge to urinate had come on strong. Normally I could conduct a five second wrap-up of whatever I was doing and make it to the restroom, no problem. But suddenly, within literal seconds of first experiencing the urge, there was no stopping it.

My dark trousers kept the secret after I left the room, and I was able to slip back into the then-empty conference room later to clean up under the guise that I had "spilled my coffee." But as I pled sudden illness and left work early, I began taking inventory of my life. The sudden and frequent need to urinate had been going on for the last two years. I was living an embarrassing stream of television ads almost all featuring men and women twice my age. But my problem had become unmanageable. I made an appointment with my first doctor since childhood for the next day.

My doctor did not recoil in horror when I told him why I'd come. Instead he talked me through a series of questions and even made a "gotta go" joke that was deeply appreciated during this awkward conversation about public urination. He ran tests for Parkinson's, multiple sclerosis and diabetes, all of which came back negative. He prescribed me pills that didn't do much to ease my discomfort or lessen my risk of what was rapidly becoming frequent accidents.

I began a year-long and seemingly endless tour of urologists, gastroenterologists and specialists of every body part you could imagine. I was finally diagnosed with "idiopathic overactive bladder:" a nice way of saying, "This guy constantly has to urinate for no good reason." By this time, I was spending my life in a state of abject horror. What had been an outgoing personality shriveled up. I went to work but spoke little. I stopped meeting with friends. I stopped dating. I retreated from life. I took too many sick days so I didn't have to face what was happening. Three years since it started, I was laid off.

Suddenly, with no solution to my problem in sight, and a life I was shocked to discover had become lonely and disengaged, I moved back in with my mother and father. They were overcome as they learned the extent of my plight. One day, they sat down with me in my lived-in bedroom and produced a packet. On the cover was one giant word, "Botox." I knew what Botox was and as I understood it, it helped keep celebrities looking young. Plastic surgery was the least of my worries, and the fact that my parents were suggesting it suddenly made me wonder if they were trying to shame me out of their house completely.

But then my mother tapped a series of words inside the pamphlet. "As little as 100 units injected into the bladder can help ease the spasms of the detrusor muscle that often leads to overactive bladder (OVB)." I remembered having heard about an injection treatment having had some success in Europe, but it still hadn't been approved in the U.S.

"It was approved in January," my mother said, as if she was reading my mind.

The absurdity and shame that had already made up the majority of my 20s was about to hit a whole new low. In the doctor's office with the packet in hand, I found I couldn't even find the words. But when he saw me he smiled and led the way. That day, my bladder was scheduled for some much-needed plastic surgery, and my life changed forever.

The procedure was an uncomfortable one, and unfortunately must be repeated quarterly. But my life over the subsequent year quietly changed into one in which I felt normal again, even confident. I got another job as an aide in the mayor's office, and I started dating again. Soon, I was able to move out of my parents' house and follow up on all the dreams I had had before all of this began—including law school.

My life lessons from OAB, as you can imagine, are many. I find that very little embarrasses me anymore. I am grateful for my life and my newfound ability to live it. I have learned that my condition was very likely caused by alcohol consumption in college, and as such, I have been completely sober for two years. In fact, a total shift in my diet has similarly helped alleviate my symptoms to such a degree that my doctors feel I might be able to go off the Botox eventually and begin a small regimen of a new oral medication.

My goals are to live a normal life and to accomplish my myriad dreams knowing that I have overcome an obstacle that is, frankly, much too embarrassing to put into a personal essay for a law school application—which is exactly why I am putting it here. I have learned not to be ashamed of what I have dealt with; I have learned that it makes me who I am today, someone who can empathize with others when their struggles are taboo, and someone who can face what has made me and say, I will keep working toward my dreams.

JDMISSION REVIEW

Overall Lesson

The story that is most meaningful to you may not be the best topic for your personal statement.

First Impression

Despite the essay's slightly uncomfortable topic, I think it has a strong beginning. I am curious to see where the candidate goes with it.

Strengths

The candidate seems generally intelligent, and I am sympathetic to his plight. The writing is good overall, though the ending of the essay leaves something to be desired, as does the subject matter.

Weaknesses

This is an odd essay. Again, I am not sure what to make of its primary subject matter. I certainly wonder if this really was the "best" story the candidate could have chosen to share, but at the same time, that is precisely his point—the topic is taboo, yet he refuses to be embarrassed by it. I am left wondering if perhaps the topic would be better suited to an addendum essay explaining the gap on his resume.

If the candidate ultimately opts to stick with this theme, I think he could tell the story of what happened in fewer words and devote more attention to the *meaning* of it: that he grew as a person through the experience and, as a result, will enter law school with a more challenging personal history and a more empathetic outlook. This is a profound point he could make, and although he does touch on it, he does not express it as fully and effectively as he could. And rather than discussing his bladder troubles for more than a full page, he should shift the essay's focus away from the minute details of his story and instead reflect on the overall experience.

Finally, the candidate needs to explain his motivation for pursuing a law degree. He mentions his past employment as a paralegal and implies that attending law school was one of his dreams before his medical problem wreaked havoc on his life. However, he never actually discusses why he is interested in becoming a lawyer, so this missing information needs to be added.

Final Assessment

As an initial exercise, I would encourage this candidate to brainstorm other possible topics just to see what alternate options might exist. He does not necessarily *need* to change topics; this one could still work with some major revisions. To make this an effective essay, however, the candidate must situate the topic within a richer, more nuanced, and concise reflection on why this experience is such a significant part of his path to law school. Remember, the purpose of your personal statement is to convince the admissions office that it *wants* you at its school. What is the very best material you have to accomplish that goal?

PERSONAL STATEMENT 10

Pick a theme and stick with it.

"Cease fire, cease fucking fire! I said cease fucking fire Privates!" As I put my M4 rifle on safe mode and pointed the muzzle downward, I looked to my left and right toward my battle buddies at the United States Army infantry basic training. As soon as I turned my head to where all the drill sergeants were gathered, I felt a chill running down my back. A week prior, one of my battle buddies was shot in the head during a training course called "NIC at Night." This time, it was a suicide. In my head I heard, "Why am I here? Why did I choose to be an infantryman? I don't want to die."

I took my first step in America when I was twelve years old with a Mickey Mouse backpack on my back and two gigantic suitcases in both of my hands. In my pocket contained two good-bye letters written by my parents in Korea. My Korean-American legal guardians welcomed me to America with a big friendly "Hello!" I didn't know the language but recognized the phrase from television. Everything changed once I stepped into their home. At dinner tables, I mastered the skill of quickly grabbing and eating food from dishes while they looked away. I mastered hiding my money and keeping a spending record, because it would "disappear" otherwise. I mastered leaving good impression on my friends' mothers so that they would give me rides home to my drunk guardian. And I mastered deceiving my parents over the phone, so they would not worry.

I was not, however, able to master the skill of ignoring the sceneries of families eating out at restaurants. I used to have reoccurring dreams of chasing after my parents and my sister, but no matter how hard I ran toward them, I could not get any closer.

When I was sixteen, my parents and older sister joined me in this country. I was finally able to wake up everyday to the smell of my mother's cooking and the sound of my father and sister waking up. The sights of families eating out at restaurants no longer made me sad. I could not ask for anything more.

There is a saying in Korean, "The moment when you put your guard down is the moment you get hurt." When I left for college, my parents' fights increased while my sister's depression worsened. It broke my heart to see my sister sitting in a wheelchair one day, her hair all over the place, refusing to see any of us at the hospital. After a series of other heartbreaking events, my father left our family.

It was then that I chose to become an Infantryman for the United States Army National Guard. Before I left for basic training, I pictured myself being free from all the family responsibilities back at home. But a different kind of responsibility awaited me at basic training. As a squad leader, it was my duty to care for those under me before caring for myself. If there was not enough food, I had to let the men under me eat first, settling for very small portions. And if the security shifts did not allow all of my squad to get sleep, I had to yield my sleeps to others. We were all family; there were no "I's." If one person made a mistake, we all received punishment. If one person achieved a merit, we all received the award.

One morning, it was about 0600 and we were ruck-marching with eighty pounds of equipment on our bodies. After awhile, our platoon found ourselves carrying and passing around an extra rucksack of a battle buddy who could barely march anymore. Our chain was only as strong as our weakest link.

In the rank of Specialist today, I make sure that the privates are consistently improving as infantrymen, and I engage in their personal lives to make sure they are not experiencing any troubles outside of their uniforms. Through all of my experience in basic training, I learned to accept my life back at home. It was on me to make the weakest link in our family chain become stronger, and to this day I believe that about my role in my family.

I know I will approach the challenges of law school in this same way—with an intention of improving those around me by improving myself. Today, there are many soldiers who are going through more trying difficulties than I have, and those soldiers, including the wounded veterans, in some instances have trouble legally representing themselves. I plan to become a JAG officer in the United States Army to become a voice for my brothers and sisters in arms.

jdMission Review

Overall Lesson

Be sure that when you tell a story in your essay—especially a great one—it fits somehow into your statement's overall theme.

First Impression

I am enthralled and want to continue reading to learn more about this candidate and his experience in the military. I also see moments of promise in his writing ability, at least initially.

Strengths

This essay contains some beautiful, sincere moments. I love the detail about his Mickey Mouse backpack. I love the heartbreaking genuineness of this sentence: "I used to have reoccurring dreams of chasing after my parents and my sister, but no matter how hard I ran toward them, I could not get any closer."

In particular, the following statements illustrate a powerful link between his background/home life and his military experience: "Through all of my experience in basic training, I learned to accept my life back at home. It was on me to make the weakest link in our family chain become stronger, and to this day I believe that about my role in my family." That said, he misses an opportunity to flesh this idea out (though he would need to do so briefly, given that this essay is already long) by adding a sentence or two to clarify the following: How did his behavior change when he moved back home? How did he treat and view his family differently?

Weaknesses

In some places, the candidate's writing is awkward, and he regularly uses words incorrectly. For example, the word "sceneries" does not mean what he thinks in this sentence: "I was not, however, able to master the skill of ignoring the sceneries of families eating out at restaurants." He means "scenes of," which is better than "sceneries," but "sight" would be even better. And even though the numerous grammar and spelling issues throughout the essay may not be problematic enough to warrant a rejection, they can be distracting to the reader and thereby lessen the impact of the stories he is sharing.

Further, I am a little confused by this sentence: "It broke my heart to see my sister sitting in a wheelchair one day, her hair all over the place, refusing to see any of us at the hospital." If she would not allow him to visit, how could he have seen what she looked like at the time? Although I can imagine what the explanation for this might be, a little clarification would prevent the reader from becoming confused, which is another distraction.

Finally, by the end of the essay, I am not quite sure what the overall statement's theme is. For example, I do not know why the candidate introduced his family. He should find a way to somehow incorporate the discussion of his family and the redefinition of his familial role into how he views his future legal career.

Final Assessment

This candidate's essay includes a lot of great material. If he added a few sentences to connect his military experience with his family experience and to explain how these experiences relate in turn to his law school aspirations, his personal statement would read more coherently in terms of theme and overall message.

PERSONAL STATEMENT 11

Contextualize specific passions.

I don't imagine the process of coming out as gay is easy for anyone. I can still remember the first time the words came out of my mouth. The person I told, my best friend, waited expectantly for the big news I had promised her over the phone. My heart began to beat faster. My palms were sweating. A million thoughts raced through my head. Here was something integral to my identity, something so deep it had taken me years to uncover. And I was about to tell someone who could either accept it, or turn away from me.

Fortunately, the experience in my case was a positive one, overall. Without fail, my closest friends and family told me they loved me, and would continue to do so. There were, of course, some people who did not accept me, and that hurt in ways that I can't begin to explain. But the ones who really mattered embraced me, and coming out to them was an affirming experience. I knew even more than I had before that I had a network of people around me who cared for me and supported me.

When I was in college, I became involved in activities that affirmed my identity further. I organized on campus for things like a gay student union and gender non-specific bathrooms, and the groups I worked with had various levels of success with these projects. But [my undergraduate university] is a largely queer-friendly school in New York City, and so the activities felt somewhat sheltered. After organizing with these campus groups for a while, I branched out and began volunteering for organizations in the city at large.

I had always known that not everyone's experience of coming out as gay was as positive as mine, but it was when I became involved with these organizations that I began to see just how cruel the world could be to LGBTQIA [lesbian, gay, bisexual, transgender, questioning, intersex, and asexual] people. I met thirteen-year-olds who had been abused and thrown into the street because they were gay. I met trans women who had been discriminated against for their identities by bosses and landlords. I met drag queens whose daily experience involved street harassment and the threat of bodily harm. For the first time in my life I was surrounded by people who were struggling every day to meet their basic needs like food and shelter because of their identities.

I also began to learn from people who were older than me, who had slept on the Chelsea Piers, and lived through the plague of HIV and AIDS. I learned about intersectionality, the varied forms that oppression can take and where they meet in an individual's life. I learned of how mainstream organizations like HRC [Human Rights Campaign] and those involved in the fight for marriage equality often jettison the most vulnerable members of queer struggle in order to achieve what they consider the "greater good"—like the exclusion of transgender people from the Employment Non-Discrimination Act in the '90s. I learned about assimilation of gay people into mainstream society, and how it worked remarkably well for some while for others it would never, ever be an option.

In the end, it was these—the most vulnerable members of my community—that I found the most reason to fight for. People whose doctors won't treat them because they're HIV positive. Trans men and trans women without legal documentation who can't find a lawyer that will take them on. Intersex prisoners who the prison industrial complex tries to squeeze into its limited boxes.

I honestly believe going to law school is the best way I can help these people. I have spent years writing and signing petitions, organizing LGBTQIA dance parties, protesting in the streets. Now, as I enter the phase of my life in which I am choosing a profession, I want it to be one that takes all I have learned and keeps it in the forefront of my mind. I want to stand up for the people in my community who have so few advocates.

A queer utopia—that is, a world in which the struggles I have learned of through my involvement in the LGBTQIA community no longer exist—is still a long way off. But I have seen good people filling in the gaps in the lives of those most strongly affected by inequality. I am committed to becoming one of those people, and I feel that this is the best way I can do it.

jdMission Review

Overall Lesson

If you are passionate about a specific issue, that is fine—but take a moment to step back and contextualize it in a sentence or two.

First Impression

After reading the first paragraph, I completely forgot to stop to jot down my first impression, which I think is a great sign. I read the entire essay before I remembered to document my initial impression, and I believe this speaks to the essay's strength.

Strengths

This candidate is one of my favorite kinds of applicants and one admissions officers seem to appreciate as well—she has the experience to support what she claims are her passions, she demonstrates her sincerity by sharing insight and knowledge she has gained from her experiences, and she offers reflections that reveal her capacity for intellectual thought. Here is a specific example of what I mean: "I met thirteen-year-olds who had been abused and thrown into the street because they were gay. I met trans women who had been discriminated against for their identities by bosses and landlords. I met drag queens whose daily experience involved street harassment and the threat of bodily harm. For the first time in my life I was surrounded by people who were struggling every day to meet their basic needs like food and shelter because of their identities."

She then goes on to do the same on a broader scale: "I learned of how mainstream organizations like HRC and those involved in the fight for marriage equality often jettison the most vulnerable members of queer struggle in order to achieve what they consider the 'greater good'—like the exclusion of transgender people from the Employment Non-Discrimination Act in the '90s."

Overall, these kinds of sentences persuade the reader that the candidate is who she says she is, and they convey that her desire to attend law school is heartfelt, as is her interest in a specific kind of legal career.

Weaknesses

This essay holds together well. My only criticism might be that adding a passage of neutral analysis would be beneficial in breaking up this block of righteous-rage text. I do not mean that the candidate should water down her fervent energy, which is in no small part driven by anger, but her essay could be more profound if she were to step back from her enthusiasm for a moment and reflect even *more* broadly on the implications of her topic. I am referring to the theme of injustice in general and how a society deals with it over time, or perhaps how various societies now view and have historically viewed gender—and how all these realities intersect with liberty and oppression. Although I thoroughly enjoyed this essay as is, I still think it could use a few sentences from a more distant, bird's-eye view that contextualize contemporary LGBTQIA issues within the larger framework of American history.

In addition, the candidate's use of the abbreviation LGBTQIA without any definition or explanation was slightly jarring, because I did not know what the "I" and "A" represent. I had to go look the extended abbreviation up. She likewise references the organization HRC without providing any other details or the group's full name. When you use an abbreviation that your reader cannot readily understand, your statement loses some impact. Either your reader must stop and do additional work to get the full effect of your text (by looking up the abbreviation, as I had to do), or he/she will simply read on without doing so, meaning that some of your intended meaning will likely be lost. You will save admissions officers time and energy—and ensure that you keep their uninterrupted attention—by always explaining or writing out any abbreviations that may be unfamiliar to them.

Final Assessment

I would have a conversation with this candidate about the contextual issue I discussed earlier. I imagine she already has insights that would be easy to incorporate, perhaps just before the essay's penultimate paragraph. With a little work and some clarification of the abbreviations, this essay could be quite powerful.

PERSONAL STATEMENT 12

Push your theme to its full potential.

As promised, David got me up at eight-thirty in the morning, though I was probably already awake when he came to rouse me. It was during a summer break from college, and I had slept on his couch after a gig ran too late for me to catch the bus back to New Jersey. We'd had a late night and it was a small couch; eight-thirty felt plenty early to get up for an English soccer match. Not expecting to spend the night in the city, I hadn't even brought a change of clothes, so I was still uncomfortably clad in my now-rumpled suit as we walked over to Ali's apartment.

Ali, who grew up in Ramallah, was David's classmate at one of the grad schools at my university. We had never met, but I knew him as the frequent author of opinion pieces about the Israeli-Palestinian conflict in the campus newspaper, pieces I found quite radical in their criticism of the Israeli government. Ali held the principle of a Jewish state to be fundamentally racist and morally indefensible. As the child of an Israeli immigrant and an American Jew who felt differently, to say the least, I was offended by what seemed to be attacks on the morality of my family. I imagined Ali to be a nasty guy, or at least someone hopelessly biased and embittered by his Palestinian background. That is, someone I wouldn't necessarily choose to hang out with on a Saturday morning. It didn't ease my apprehension when David, spotting my Israeli souvenir keychain as we gathered our things to set out, said, "Better not let Ali see that, mate."

Yet the grinning, boyish figure in a too-large Liverpool jersey that greeted us when we arrived scarcely resembled the snarling antagonist of my mind's eye. Once he had got us comfortably seated in front of the television, he slipped into the kitchen and reemerged just in time for the match's opening whistle with an enormous tray of food. The spread was astonishing: fresh scrambled eggs and bacon ("Good Muslim," he said with a sheepish smile; "Good Jew," I agreed), bowls of potato chips and pretzels, even a platter of miniature hamburgers. There was hot coffee and cold beer. It was nine in the morning; how early had he risen to prepare all that? It was far more than the three of us could possibly finish.

So we gorged ourselves on greasy food as we watched the game, swapping stories and jokes and arguing congenially about soccer. I can't recall whether the game was a good one, or even who was playing (though probably Liverpool was involved), but my mind returns often to Ali's hospitality that morning. I arrived at his apartment with not only a stranger's typical discomfort but also a specific set of negative and condescending prejudgments. The warm welcome I received made me realize what now seems obvious: that my attitude had been immature; that Ali's opinions, right or wrong, were worth engaging with sincerely on the level of rational argument, rather than dismissing as the product of spite or dishonesty; that my upbringing made me every bit as vulnerable to bias on these issues as his made him. In fact, I had formed assumptions about him that I had never held about people whose views offended me from the opposite (i.e., "pro-Israel") extreme, but whose familial or cultural background more closely resembled my own.

Ali treated me with unconditional kindness and respect merely because I was a guest in his home, while in my private reaction to his articles I had not been as charitable. Not only was I guilty of the intellectually compromising impulse to dismiss the character of someone with whom I disagreed; I also felt that I had wronged Ali personally by conflating his political stance with his humanity. It was fortunate that his overwhelming hospitality and affability disabused me of my preconceptions. But I can't always count on a smiling Palestinian with a tray of hamburgers to make me aware of the need to maintain an open mind. I have to try to channel Ali's graciousness into all my dealings with others, particularly those whose beliefs grate against mine. Of course I sometimes fail to live up to this ideal—who knows, maybe Ali does, too—but it is a worthy aspiration.

jdMission Review

Overall Lesson

Go beyond yourself where you can.

First impression

The first paragraph is simply the beginning of a story—it includes no topic sentence at all. This is a bit unusual in personal statements, but the writing is good, and I am curious to know where he will go from here.

Strengths

The description of the spread in the third paragraph serves the story perfectly. Going into such detail about the food conveys the level of preparation necessary to provide such a feast, and we pick up on where the applicant is going: he is going to feel like a jerk. When he does, it is earned.

The ultimate lesson—that we should not conflate humanity with politics—is smart and portrays the candidate as an empathetic person capable of high-level thought.

Weaknesses

The first paragraph sets the scene well—we want to know what happens next—but it includes details that turn out to be irrelevant. Why do we need to know that he is rumpled and tired? Perhaps his dishevelment renders his propensity to make assumptions a bit more understandable. After all, he is exhausted. So he may have included these details for just that reason, but I am dubious that fatigue and assumption-making are linked. People who get plenty of sleep can carry terrible biases, and people who do not may be the most open-minded folks on the planet. The connection is a weak one at best. Better to set a scene with details that pertain directly to the lesson: the keychain is a great example.

105

He is also walking a fine line with respect to what constitutes an assumption. In the story, this particular person (Ali) has written opinions that the candidate felt were "attacks on the morality of [his] family." We do not know the tone of this person's op-eds, but if it was angry, then assuming that he is an angry man by nature seems fairly reasonable. A stronger way to address this may be to make the "assumption" not about Ali as a person but about how the two of them would relate: "I assumed that we were not going to get along." This way, the applicant makes an assumption about a dynamic based on both parties' political views rather than on one person's suspected personality. Otherwise, the writer's assumption could come across as either ignorant (if it is ill-founded) or not a very big deal (if it is not actually that crazy). We all make assumptions—some are just dumber than others. He does not want to make himself seem too biased or stupid; "old selves" that are that way tend to come across as exaggerated.

Finally, although this personal statement has a great take-away, the applicant could do more with it. The take-away statement appears in the middle of the last paragraph: "I had wronged Ali personally by conflating his political stance with his humanity." With this sentence, the applicant expresses a profound and important idea, and he does so in a way that feels sincere based on everything we have read to this point. However, he stops himself too early. What he is describing—the tendency to make assumptions—is remarkably common. It could therefore lead him to think even bigger: how does a society deal with this phenomenon? How might law?

Final Assessment

The essay's theme seems to be that even though doing so is inevitable, we should strive to not make assumptions and to keep an open mind. It is a feel-good take-away, and he writes convincingly about the incident that led him to it, but he could go further. As a law school applicant, he could let us know why this matters to him—when many people in a community or culture think a certain way, what does that mean for society? How do we design and apply laws around it? These questions would have taken this essay from strong to even better.

Personal Statement 13

Portray yourself in a way that
serves your purpose.

My name is Min-Jae but I go by MJ. I am not trying to Americanize my Korean roots with this nickname. In fact, I am deeply proud of them. I was born in Irvine, CA, so by virtue of circumstance I am American. But my soul is Korean, even if my dance moves are 100% MJ – *Michael Jackson.*

When I was twelve, I discovered that not only could I dance, but I had *moves.* It was at Eliza Kravitz's Bat Mitzvah that for the first time people took notice. "Hot in Here" by Nelly started blasting through the Music King's speakers, as the dry ice machine kicked it into high gear. I burst onto the dance floor. Then I just started to move. I saw a popular kid named Stan Larson move out of my way which was in his best interest. Suddenly the song ended and when my faculties returned, the whole Bat Mitzvah party was screaming. At first I couldn't tell what their enthusiasm was about. And then it became clear. It was about me! The dance floor had literally circled up to watch me dance, and now they were cheering. I left the floor, but my heart stayed back there, forever twelve and dancing to Nelly.

That's what dancing is for me. It's a forgetting of the world and a return to a primal self. I make sure to dance at least once a day. In my opinion, people who go to the gym are wasting time and money. They could just play a beloved Brittany, Madonna or Michael Jackson number and let loose until they've danced their way into a healthy body and mind.

Soon after, I adopted the name MJ. Even my parents called me MJ. They understood that it wasn't a slight against their motherland, but an homage to my biggest idol. I perfected moves like the Moonwalk and The Anti-Gravity Lean. I became so good at the Toe Stand that it was often requested at parties and even just randomly walking down the halls of my high school. Dancing was such a fundamental part of me, that when I got to college I was overcome with profound emptiness. Who was I without this integral part of my personality on display?

So, I made a plan. I set up speakers in the hall. Then that night around 9PM when a lot of the kids were sitting around, I cranked up the Michael Jackson classic, "Don't Stop 'Til You Get Enough," and I danced my way down the hall. At first no one knew what to make of me. But by the end, I had them. Everyone was clapping and dancing along. After that, everyone knew my name.

My first job out of college was working for an events company as a caterer. I believed I was perfectly suited to events where everyone is dancing or about to dance. Unfortunately, very quickly I learned that I couldn't easily be a part of it. Sure I could dance in the kitchen once the door swung closed. But then the noise from the appliances and the rest of the staff made it tough to hear the music.

I only worked five events before I had to give up the job. Perhaps it sounds dramatic, but it felt so important for me to be able to release my urge to dance, that the first time the music played and I didn't even feel the urge? I had to get out. It was too much to handle. I finished out the night and drove myself home where I played "Beat It" with the volume turned up loud.

I began to rehearse for the show <u>So You Think You Can Dance</u>. Finally, the audition day came. I waiting in the line for more than seven hours, not counting the four I spent in line before the auditions even began. And then, as I stood before Shane Sparks and the other judges, I heard my song, "Bad," come up and I made my move. When it was over they said, "MJ, like Michael," and they high fived me. They said, "For a skinny kid, you sure can dance!" I went through to the next round, but as I stood there, something wasn't right. I couldn't feel the music, which was "Smooth Criminal." I danced my heart out, but it didn't feel right and I knew before they even said the words that I wasn't going to move on to the next round. I was glad I got to try, but it didn't seem like dancing as a career was going to happen for me.

Over the last several months I have considered what I want to do with my life. I know that I am a dancer, but I can be a dancer no matter what I do. Whether I'm going to school, serving at formal events or even dancing on a reality TV show. I know that as a lawyer I can work in the entertainment world, helping other dancers to live their dreams. And I know that I can dance in my heart the whole time I am doing it.

JDMISSION REVIEW

Overall Lesson

Remember, your goal in writing your personal statement is to reveal something meaningful about yourself—not to just tell a cute story.

First Impression

I like the first paragraph, but the end of it makes me a bit nervous. I wonder, "Is he actually going to write a personal statement about his great dance skills?" I am half charmed and half anxious.

Strengths

The candidate comes across as playful and spirited, and his essay is interesting and enjoyable to read. Apart from these aspects, however, it offers little of substance for an admissions officer.

Weaknesses

If this candidate had a 180 LSAT score and a 3.9 GPA, *maybe* he could submit this essay and be accepted to law school. However, the chances of someone reading this essay and thinking, "Now here's someone who will make a great lawyer" are slim.

I am not saying that he strikes me as unintelligent—just a little out of the ordinary. And more importantly, he is still a mystery to me even after I have read the entire essay. I do not know anything about him except that he loves to dance. Nothing. Maybe he believes that nothing else about him is worth sharing, but if that is the case, why does he aspire to attend law school?

Final Assessment

I would start from scratch with this candidate. First, I would assign him an "identities" exercise in which he would step back and consider *all* the identities he has as MJ—not just a dancer, but a son, a friend, a former caterer, etc. Then we would discuss personal stories related to these identities that reveal more about him as a potential law student and lawyer than just his love of dancing.

Personal Statement 14

Lose the melodrama.

I was born into a one-car family that didn't use disposable diapers or paper towels, and that counted literal squares of toilet paper. My mother's bent was toward making everything as difficult as possible to throw away. I resented it, because the effort felt too tiny, too pockmarked by the indifference of the rest of the world. The fact that I didn't use paper products meant nothing within the greater scope of existence. 165,000 new cars designed to use gas were still being produced everyday. By the time I left for college, the ideals of my parents had become deeply buried beneath the allure of ease and indulgence.

After I graduated from business school with an economics degree, I worked for three years as a banker on Wall Street, as soulless and blood-sucking a profession as the cliché Hollywood and grassroots movements have contrived. I made money hand-over-fist in my first year alone and bought new suits when I didn't have time to get the old ones cleaned. I drank bourbon and snorted coke after work. I drank coke and snorted bourbon during work. The meaninglessness of every step I took stalked me like a shadow.

Then one night I woke up, twenty-four years old and already older than my grandfather. I stared into the vacuous holes in my head masquerading as eyes as sweat poured in rivulets around them. I picked up a pen, sat down and wrote out my manifesto. It was the beginning of something vast. By the time I had finished it, the day had slipped by. There were messages on my phone from my colleagues, my bosses and my mother. I didn't call any of them back. I read and re-read my manifesto. I debated mailing it to the media, my sister, Gawker, or The Times. Then I went to sleep.

The manifesto proclaimed, in part:

> It's easy to get ensnared by the suggested importance of man-made constructs like wealth and pretty-things. But the truth is that the goal of all life is survival. And I see before us a violent and manufactured death. There is no nature in death by fossil fuel. There is no nature in death by garbage heap. There is no nature in death by deoxygenating our planet. There is no nature in death by war.

Nature lives in the majesty of clean rivers, full trees, minimal waste, green fuels and the potential we each have to change our own fate. I hereby dedicate my life to changing the fate of the world. If I have to murder, decree or reconfigure the laws of the land, so be it. I owe it to myself, humanity and life itself, as each of us does. I move forward with a mind that fights, that has purpose. There is no passion in my thought or deed, but rather, a mission that is clear and principled. It begins today.

I slept for a while. When I finally awoke, I felt like something akin to lifeblood was regenerating in a modest trickle through my veins. I quit my job. I moved back to my parents' house, the one in which I had grown up. I went back into my childhood room where my brother's Star Trek posters hung next to my Raider's poster signed by Hall of Famer, Marcus Allen. I re-connected with a primal, formative part of myself that had been stripped over the years, layer by layer.

I began a deep and intoxicating study of the technologies already changing the world and considered how to make them the only option. "Outlaw fossil fuels," a voice whispered. The same way we protect the elephant by outlawing the sale and manufacture of ivory, let's protect the remaining stores of coal and oil.

The more I understood the rules of the world, the better I understood how to change them. I sought out legal counsel, intricately studied the path of our nation's finest environmental lawyers. I studied thousands of drop movers, men and women grasping for buckets of water of change, and only getting a single drip across the finish line.

I began to assess the best way to make bold and blanketing moves. I did not intend to be a drop mover— I wanted to open the floodgates. I realized I would have to begin again. Although my intention to change things grows ever more urgent as glaciers break off into the oceans, it now has become morbidly clear that the change must take place within institutions that are already in place. I intend to be the kind of environmental lawyer that changes things by the ocean-full.

There is no time left. I am ready to turn my manifesto into action points. I am ready to save the world. I hope when I get into law school, your halls are teeming with people just like me: filled with purpose, ready for change, and able to fulfill the manifold dreams of our planet.

JDMISSION REVIEW

Overall Lesson

Convey passion, but not at the expense of reason.

First Impression

The first paragraph could be a little confusing. My initial impression from the list of behaviors presented in the first sentence (having just one car, counting sheets of toilet paper, etc.) was that the candidate's family was poor, not that it was environmentally conscious. However, he could easily clarify this point by saying that his family adopted these behaviors as part of its environmentally conscious lifestyle.

Strengths

Parts of this essay contain some really nice phrasing. "The meaninglessness of every step I took stalked me like a shadow," for example, struck me as a lovely articulation of the candidate's feelings. It also provides a strong ending for that paragraph by striking the right tone, invoking a powerful visual image, and setting the stage for the candidate's life-changing decision, revealed in the next section of his personal statement.

I also believe that the candidate sincerely wants to go to law school—and for the reasons he gives later in the essay.

Weaknesses

The phrase "snorted bourbon" does not work for me. I know the candidate is trying to be clever with words, but the physical impossibility of what he is describing overshadows the wordplay. Consider also the sentence "Then one night I woke up, twenty-four-years old and already older than my grandfather," which is unquestionably poetic. However, because this is a personal statement and the rest of the information the candidate is sharing is not hyperbolic (except the part about snorting bourbon), I think he needs to temper the metaphor with reality just a bit. He still can make the same suggestion—that he had aged dramatically for a 24-year-old—but he should adjust the metaphor to make it less literal. For example, he could say something like, "Then one night I woke up, 24 years old, with the resigned cloudiness of my grandfather." Or he could use a phrase like "hard-won fatigue" or "stale weariness" instead of "resigned cloudiness"—whatever the candidate prefers, but without jarring the reader with such a sudden stylistic shift.

Along similar lines, but for a different (and perhaps obvious) reason, he needs to cut the parts where he says he snorted coke and will commit murder. Do not casually allude to your criminal behavior, past or future, in your personal statement.

Final Assessment

In addition to making the edits I suggest in the Weaknesses section, I would advise this candidate to tone down his language in a few places. For example, he should probably reconsider the term "manifesto"—it just sounds a bit too *Mein Kampf*-y to me. I also think he should remove the phrase "save the world" from the last paragraph to avoid being overly dramatic. This candidate is great at conveying passion (ironically, and a bit confusedly, since he claims to lack it), but he also needs to impart that he is a reasoned individual.

Personal Statement 15

Vary your sentence structure.

On December 19, 1996, at the age of five, I lost five close family members in a house fire. The oldest victim was my 10-year-old aunt. She and I grew up together, living in my grandmother's apartment in the [housing projects] in South Central Los Angeles. After losing my aunt and my other family members in the fire, I became depressed. Suddenly, being the only child in my grandmother's home, without any other children to talk to or play with, I developed imaginary friends. Because I talked to these "friends," my grandmother advised my mother to find a psychiatrist for me. My mother, however, ignored my grandmother's advice because she understood my behavior as a coping mechanism for the trauma I had experienced. After my aunt's death, I felt a profound sense of emptiness; yet, over time, I filled that void by helping others.

I believe the best way I can help people is through the legal system. I chose this route when I began noticing the injustices occurring in my community. When my friends and family interacted with authorities, they were often treated unfairly. Unfortunately, many people in my South Central Los Angeles community did not understand their rights and did not know how to represent or stand up for themselves. My uncle Edward, my Aunt Donna's younger brother, was falsely convicted on the basis of planted evidence. If only my uncle had known his rights and how to seek effective legal representation, he would probably not have a felony on his record today. My uncle's situation showed me that ignorance of one's rights can lead to prejudicial treatment in the American legal system, and I realized that educating the members of my community would make them less vulnerable. I will work to expose such injustices and focus on corrective measures for all Americans because no one deserves unfair treatment.

Disenfranchised Americans receive unequal treatment in the legal system when they are accused of crimes and when they are victims of crimes. During my internship at the Department of Justice Community Relations Service (CRS) in Washington D.C., I discovered the case of Jason Smith, a fourteen-year-old African American boy who was brutally murdered by the Ku Klux Klan in Louisiana in June of 2011. This case was not processed in a timely manner because one of the alleged murderers was the son of a former FBI agent. Once I knew that this case coincided with the CRS' goal to resolve community tensions and conflicts, I submitted a written report to the Acting National Director of the division, who reviewed the report and informed me that no one in the CRS Headquarters or regional offices had been aware of this incident. She forwarded my report to the regional director in Louisiana to further research the case because the hate crime had occurred within that jurisdiction. I later learned that the Civil Rights Division was investigating the murder.

The Jason Smith case particularly interested me because my younger brother, Kevin, was the same age as Jason when Jason died. When I look at Kevin and see his bright future, it saddens me to know that a child's murder can go unnoticed. I feel relieved and gratified that I could make a difference by highlighting the injustice of Jason's murder. Jason and my uncle's situation reinforced my commitment to the practice of law. As an attorney, I will expose and speak out against injustices. By providing closure for families experiencing injustices and making the legal process comprehensible to those who are unfamiliar with it, I will help bridge the justice gap between socially marginalized individuals and the larger American society. I want to help the disenfranchised feel less excluded from the mainstream world. I can contribute to this by helping ensure that everyone receives effective legal representation.

My involvement with the Jason Smith case at CRS helped me realize that my work in the legal system can effect real change in the lives of people from underprivileged communities. The [target law school's legal clinic] will provide me with the foundation that I need to become an outstanding advocate. Participating in this clinic will improve my knowledge of civil procedures and enable me to provide legal services to underrepresented communities. My cultural sensitivity and open-mindedness will make it easier for clients from these communities to open up and enable me to effectively communicate with them. My leadership ability, organizational skills, and tenacity make me a resource to the [law school's] community. Additionally, my discipline and dedication, along with my desire to make my Aunt Donna proud, will motivate me to persevere through the rigors of law school. I will contribute my commitment to success, my ability to work with diverse groups, my inner-city urban perspective, and most importantly, my optimism to the [law school].

JDMISSION REVIEW

Overall lesson

Vary your sentence length to keep readers interested, and do not assume they can read your mind.

First Impression

After I read the first sentence, my reaction was simply "wow." Her first paragraph proceeds in equally compelling fashion.

Strengths

Overall, this personal statement is excellent. The candidate discusses a significant accomplishment in her life and what it meant to her personally, given her uncle's legal problems and her concern for her brother. The essay relates that accomplishment to her professional experience and aspirations, and it is well written and polished. If she were to send it to an admissions office today, she would be submitting a fine essay. However, she could make it even stronger.

Weaknesses

The essay is missing a transition from the candidate's experience of being a lonely child to her use of helping people as a way of filling the void created by the loss of her aunt. I do not understand how she jumped from creating imaginary friends to helping people. We need more explanation—something like, "Because I was alone, I became an independent child, a quiet observer of the world around me. I noticed things that were troubling. My uncle went to prison but claimed he did nothing wrong, and I didn't understand why. As I grew older, I began to search for a sense of purpose. When I found that helping others gave me a sense of fulfillment and eased some of my loneliness, I dove in." This is just an example of what she might write, of course, but something along these lines would strengthen that one weak spot.

Also, notice that many of the candidate's sentences are roughly the same length. You can have the most interesting content imaginable, but if your writing is too rhythmic, the reader's natural tendency is to tune out. For example, she writes, "I believe the best way I can help people is through the legal system. I chose this route when I began noticing the injustices occurring in my community. When my friends and family interacted with authorities, they were often treated unfairly." What if, instead, it read, "As a child, I began noticing that when my friends and family interacted with authorities, they were often treated unfairly. These injustices led me to decide that the best way I can help people is through the legal system"? Merely varying the sentence structure can make a big difference in keeping the reader's attention.

Final Assessment

I would advise this candidate to vary her sentence lengths a bit and to clarify the problematic transition I mentioned earlier. But again, I believe that even without these changes, she would have a solid personal statement.

PERSONAL STATEMENT 16

Steer clear of stereotypical themes.

"Good morning, Jamal, this is Ms. Smith. I am just calling to make sure that you are up and that I will see you in class at eight o'clock." This type of phone call has been a part of my morning routine for the past four years, not only for Jamal, but for all of my students who frequently arrive to school late because they have no parent or guardian at home to ensure that they arise on time. During Jamal's freshman year of high school, his father worked a night shift that prevented him from returning home until nine o'clock in the morning, and his mother lived in Jamaica, unable to move to the United States due to immigration restrictions.

While my childhood in rural Vermont revolved around helping those less fortunate, it did not prepare me to make wakeup calls to teenagers living in the tenements of New York City. Nonetheless, it was my experience volunteering for local politicians and organizations during my early home-schooling years that instilled in me a desire to explore new and illuminating environments as soon as I had the opportunity. Consequently, every morning that I make a call to one of my students, I remember why I began my career In the New York City Department of Education: to learn firsthand the inequities and injustices that affect disadvantaged populations in an urban setting, while simultaneously having a direct impact on individuals within these communities.

Jamal is only one of the more than 700 students I have educated over the past four years, but he embodies the challenges that confront many of my students. Some of the obstacles to these children's success include growing up in single-parent households, hunger, lack of basic resources, domestic violence, and language barriers. As a teacher, I have been able to mitigate many of the difficulties that my students face through making wakeup calls, keeping granola bars in my closet, having extra pencils on hand, and keeping my classroom open well after school hours. The greatest challenge I have faced as a teacher, however, has been the difficulty communicating with some of my students and their families because of a language barrier.

Over half of my students come from families whose primary language is Spanish. In attempting conversations with these individuals, I realized that the years I had spent reading and writing Spanish in academic settings did not translate into me being conversationally fluent in the language. This language impediment motivated me to travel to Guatemala this past summer. Living and conversing with a local family for three weeks, as well as traveling throughout the country on my own, allowed me to quickly gain the skills necessary to more effectively communicate with my Spanish-speaking students and their families, including Jamal's mother.

As of this fall, Jamal is the first in his family to attend college. While this is a milestone for him, his mother was unable to see him move into his dormitory, as she still lives in Jamaica and has yet to receive the immigration paperwork needed to reside in the United States. Working with Jamal and countless children from similar backgrounds has allowed me to discover how social and economic policies impact some of the country's most vulnerable populations. While my role as a teacher has allowed me to alleviate some of the difficulties that these students face, it has also made clear to me that in order to support disadvantaged populations to the extent I desire, I need to expand my knowledge of the legal system.

In pursuing a Juris Doctor, my hope is to learn how the legal system operates, while using this knowledge to assist communities similar to those I have worked with over the past four years. I believe that through involving myself with the [law school's social justice research center] and the [local justice clinic], I will best be able to do this. While I will miss greeting my students as they arrive to class on time every morning, I am certain that the knowledge and experience I will gain through [the law school]'s program will enable me to better support marginalized populations in the future.

jdMission Review

Overall Lesson

Beware of loose ends.

First Impression

Although the candidate has no way of knowing this, this kind of personal statement (based on its beginning, at least) is known among some admissions officers as the Teach for America (TFA) essay. After reading the first paragraph, I feel like I know exactly where the candidate's story is going, because I immediately assign her essay to the TFA category: She is going to say that she set out to change children's lives, but instead they changed hers. This might sound callous, but I have to say that if your current essay has a TFA theme, you should consider picking a different one—something more specific, completely different, or at least more nuanced. The "I was in fact changed" message may be 100% true, but admissions officers are tired of reading about it.

Strengths

In the second paragraph, the candidate mentions that she entered the New York City Department of Education to learn about social ills and injustice. This detail gives me a better sense of her, and I like it, though I still do not truly know who she is. In the third paragraph, we learn that she has been an educator for four years and that 700 students have passed through her doors. For me, this makes her story more impressive than I had expected—this figure demonstrates her remarkable dedication and suggests that she has exceptionally deep experience in this arena. Finally, I really like her last paragraph: it invokes her work history, summarizes nicely what she hopes to gain from her legal education, and references her target school's clinical programs specifically.

Weaknesses

That the language barrier is really the "greatest challenge" the candidate has ever faced as a teacher seems unlikely, so that claim feels too extreme. Her actual greatest challenge was probably teaching children who are living under dire circumstances how to learn and succeed. I would therefore suggest that she use slightly milder language to describe the language issue, such as referring to it as "a particularly difficult and ongoing challenge."

Plus, once the candidate begins to discuss the language issue, she changes the subject before explaining its relevance to her overall theme; therefore, it loses its power to enhance that theme. Which theme do I mean? The one buried in the last sentence of her penultimate paragraph: "While my role as a teacher has allowed me to alleviate some of the difficulties that these students face, it has also made clear to me that in order to support disadvantaged populations to the extent I desire, I need to expand my knowledge of the legal system." This is a clear summarization of what her essay is about. She needs to more directly link her language experience to her desire to help underprivileged individuals, because everything in her essay should support this theme.

Final Assessment

The candidate would benefit from revising the beginning of her essay to better convey the theme that she ultimately wants to communicate. She should go ahead and declare up front—in the very first sentence—"Being a teacher has exposed me to XYZ, and I realize that I need a law degree to deal with XYZ in the way I want." Then she can discuss the phone calls, granola bars, and language barrier. Finally, the language issue needs to play a more constructive role in the essay; it can serve as a segue to reintroducing the theme. The candidate should discuss how even mastering a new language is not enough to facilitate her goal when legal barriers still stand in the way of true solutions. This is the core reason she wants to attend law school, so she must clearly communicate that message.

Personal Statement 17

Make every illustration count.

I love gardening: My hands in the dirt, the smell of freshly grown flowers or vegetables, the invigorating sensation of working the earth in the great outdoors. There is order to sowing seeds—steps and clear directives that allow life to reproduce generationally.

I feel like the law boasts numerous similarities to a garden. While there are no hard and fast rules, there are serious guidelines to each. In a legal environment, you have to understand the existing laws of the land. But you must also understand that public opinion shifts and makes room for subtle changes to the law.

Similarly in a garden, one day it might be raining, and the next there may be a freeze. So although you might understand the rules of how to make a plant grow, you are also subject to the whims of the weather.

Every year I plant all the vegetables I like to eat in a salad. I am very specific in what I like to eat and the truth is, I only like a salad that contains each of these very specific vegetables. If one or more hasn't yet grown, I subsidize it with ones from the market. In every salad I expect:

- Lettuce

- Tomato

- Cucumber

- Radish

- Corn

More often than not, I do not have corn so I use frozen corn from the season before that I keep in my freezer. I plant corn, just as I plant lettuce, tomatoes, cucumbers, and radishes. I like the flavors as they come together: The sweetness of the corn, the juiciness of the tomato, the crunch of the cucumber, the pepper of the radish and the freshness of the lettuce. This is, to me, the perfect taste.

This is very much how I believe the law is. You bring together a specific group of rules and together they create a civilization that is preferable and comfortable and in which its citizens may thrive. For the law against drunk driving to be enough, there must be traffic laws for drivers to follow. For laws around safety there must be laws around security. For laws that protect property and finance there must be laws about how property and finance may be used.

Gardening reflects many things that are similar to the legal system. One is required to get really dirty when they garden, literally. You must dig deep in order to give your seeds the best hope of flourishing. In law, sometimes you have to dig through endless cases in order to find the seed to plant so that your jury understands your client's case.

When one gardens, one must have patience. Things don't happen immediately, even if you are re-planting something already half-grown. For the plant itself must find its roots to become a stable and thriving entity. Only then may you reap its bounty. Law is the same way. Changing the existing ways of the land takes time. The ideas must take root and grow strong and independent before you may harvest them.

It's easier to garden as a team. When I garden with my family, the garden grows bigger and stronger. In a legal team the same is true. The more brilliant minds you can bring together, the better the case you can build. But sometimes you must work alone. It can become lonely and tedious but because in one case, the vegetables are your companions and in the other, the client's story is, you aren't really ever alone. There is always a sense of accomplishment as a team.

When you sit down at the table and take a bite of the first salad of the season, you remember why life is good. When it comes to a good legal battle, the same can be true. Taking the sweet with the crunchy and peppery richness creates the perfect bite of an American salad, a dream for which my parents moved from across the sea from Ukraine to realize.

jdMission Review

Overall Lesson

Use a few strong supporting examples rather than multiple weak ones.

First Impression

I would give the first paragraph an A grade. Gardening is a rather unique subject for a personal statement, which immediately makes this essay seem potentially interesting. Also, the beginning is neither overly dramatic nor excessively dull or abstract. It strikes a good balance in that way—and this is rarer than one might think.

Strengths

I believe the essay's overall theme of comparing gardening to law can work. Although the candidate offers too many examples (as I will discuss further in the Weaknesses section of this review), the following comparisons are particularly effective:

- The similarities between the constantly shifting legal environment and the whims of the weather in the second and third paragraphs

- His discussion about the importance of patience in the eighth paragraph

- His point about how combinations of laws/plants work together in the penultimate paragraph (though this could benefit from revision by the candidate)

Weaknesses

The candidate's comparison of law to gardening would work better if he were to describe gardening first in each instance and the law second. Notice how he does the opposite at the beginning of the essay:

> I feel like the law boasts numerous similarities to a garden. While there are no hard and fast rules, there are serious guidelines to each. In a legal environment, you have to understand the existing laws of the land. But you must also understand that public opinion shifts and makes room for subtle changes to the law.

> Similarly in a garden, one day it might be raining, and the next there may be a freeze. So although you might understand the rules of how to make a plant grow, you are also a subject to the whims of the weather.

The candidate could fix this by simply changing the order of the two paragraphs.

In addition, we do not need to know what he likes to put in his salad, nor that he will not eat a salad unless it includes specific vegetables. Not only is this information superfluous, but it also makes him seem a little too compulsive.

Finally, although I actually like the idea of comparing gardening to law, the candidate provides too many comparisons. He needs to pick one or two—possibly three, if they are somewhat related—and focus on those rather than listing five or six parallels, several of which are quite weak and thereby detract from the impact of his theme.

Final Assessment

This essay essentially needs to be rewritten, though parts of it can be salvaged and used as draft material. Again, I would suggest that the candidate concentrate on fleshing out just two or three comparisons—such as the strong ones I noted in the Strengths section of this review—and eliminate the rest. However, he must be careful not to try to tell the admissions committee too much about how the law works. After all, he has not been to law school *yet*.

PERSONAL STATEMENT 18

Be realistic in how you portray
your "former" self.

I got married to a man fifteen years my senior when I was twenty years old. We had two beautiful children within two years of our wedding. When my kids turned one and two respectively, I decided to remind my husband about an agreement we'd made when we first got engaged, just as he was leaving his first marriage, and I was leaving my first year of college—that after we found a groove in our lives together, I would go back to school.

He admitted that he liked the idea of having me home with the kids, but he agreed that if we found someone we both liked and trusted to help take care of them, I should do it. My deferral period from university was coming to a close. So I immediately began my search, subsequently meeting an endless parade of absolutely suitable prospects that just weren't good enough for my babies. One thought my sister had placed in my head was, "Your kids can't yet talk, so whomever you leave them with better be above suspicion."

Of course, no one was. After weeks of searching, I debated pulling out of school. I could wait a few years until my children were older and could better indicate verbally if the babysitter was sneaking smoke breaks or serving them chocolate for lunch—or worse. Then my brother's best friend mentioned that his kids' beloved nanny was looking for a new placement. His twins were finally starting high school and her services no longer made sense for their family. My brother contacted me. And that's how Lydia came into our lives.

Lydia was two years older than me, and our chemistry was immediate. "We're going to co-parent the hell out of these monkeys," she told me, with a gentle Greek lilt in her perfect English and the loving ferocity I had been dreaming about. What's more, my kids loved her as much as we did. As our family evolved to encompass the compassionate and high-octane energy of our Lydia, for the first time in my life, I felt satisfied. I fell back into academia easily. I loved my classes and was able to study when I needed to. I had always been confident in my decision to marry and start my family young, but I suddenly had a real sense that not only could I have it all, I did.

When my son began Pre-K, he was already reading thanks to Lydia, and my three-year-old daughter could write the names of everyone in our family. Lydia was worth every cent we paid her, and we paid her well.

I take full responsibility that we never consulted Lydia about her visa status. I understand that I made a choice to pay her under-the-table when she requested it. I am fully aware that these actions were illegal. But at the time, I did not know. I was entirely unaware that when she got deported—or that that even could happen, honestly, she wasn't a criminal—my husband and I would be fined amounts that nearly equaled my student loans. To top it all off, I didn't even have a degree to help me pay off any of it, placing the financial burden squarely on the shoulders of my husband, who had absolutely no culpability in the hiring and paying of Lydia.

In the following, miserable months, my children were torn apart by the loss of Lydia. I decided that going back to school would only compound the tragedy, so I dropped out of school, my five remaining credits sitting there, not to be taken. I threw myself into being a mom and tried to repair the damage my mistake had done to my family.

Finally, my daughter was beginning first grade and my son was entering second grade. Their school offered a wonderful afterschool program. My husband and I had figured out a way to pay off those vicious fines. Lydia settled into her life in Greece, sending us letters and treats that my children treasured. We had survived the worst of it.

My husband and I talked about my loans and the possibility that now I might pursue a career. When I had been in school I was certain that career was going to be education. But now I had a different direction in mind: law. I wanted to understand the mistake I had made from the inside. From the outside, I been so childish, so immature, so misguided. Although I was voracious in my appetite to understand the unfolding events, I was still just the dumb blond who had hired the illegal alien. I was the airhead who had never thought to ask questions. I was the spoiled second wife who never paid taxes on the dog walker, the house cleaner or the gardener. Why would I pay them on the nanny? All these things were said about me. And they were true.

I am now ready to change that narrative. That's what I told my husband when I announced that now that the children were in a full day of school, I wanted to go back too. I was going to be a lawyer.

I reenrolled and finished the rest of my credits, focusing on subjects that would help to prepare me for the LSAT. I engaged in activities that would allow me to meet my newest goals. I built a new life, a knowing life, an aware life. And I grew stronger because of all of it.

JDMISSION REVIEW

Overall Lesson

Although your younger self may have been less wise than your current self, take care not to portray her as an utter fool.

First Impression

The first paragraph achieves key goals for a personal statement introduction—it is intriguing, well written, and neither overly clever nor excessively dramatic.

Strengths

This essay's strength is the story. First, the candidate effectively covers a lot of ground—from getting married and dropping out of school, to her nanny being deported, to returning to school, and ultimately to deciding to study law. She manages to convey a significant amount of information in just a few pages, and she does so without making me feel as though she is moving through her story too quickly or omitting important details. Second, the candidate does not appear to include any irrelevant material. Although I believe this essay could benefit from some trimming, that is simply because it is on the long side, not because any of the material is blatantly gratuitous. In other words, she does a good job of maintaining her focus and direction.

Weaknesses

In some places, the candidate's syntax lapses into being *too* casual—the phrase "To top it all off," for example. I do like that she writes in the same way she speaks, because this makes her writing read smoothly and sound authentic. But although the adage "write like you talk" is great for a first draft, the candidate needs to then edit that first draft to eliminate any overly informal phrases.

In addition, the section in which she relates her situation with Lydia to her law school aspirations could be improved. She writes, "I wanted to understand the mistake I had made from the inside." I buy this claim, but it is a narrow application of her experience to her interest in law. How did this ordeal affect her thoughts about immigration law? Or about herself, as someone living in the world without a clue as to how the law really works? Or about Lydia's willful violation of the law? The candidate could go in many directions with her essay, but my point is that she should pick one and go there. She needs to extend the scope of her law interest beyond simply stating that she wanted to better understand this singular experience—as true and noble as that may be.

Finally, characterizing your former self as an idiot can be dangerous. Although we were all younger and dumber once, we typically were not as dumb as we may portray ourselves for the sake of a story. Depicting your younger self as a moron is usually not a great idea, particularly when you are trying to convince a complete stranger to admit you to his/her law school. The candidate can very effectively write about what she learned from her experience without painting her younger self as entirely foolish.

Final Assessment

I would encourage this candidate to better relate the story she shares to her subsequent interest in attending law school and becoming a lawyer. She should also carefully trim and edit the language throughout her essay, paying special attention to the section in which she discusses her reaction to her poor decisions in the past and their consequences on her life and family.

Personal Statement 19

Put in the work to tell
a good story well.

After I graduated from college, I was given a fellowship to teach English in rural China. The January before I left, I attended a three-day retreat with other prospective fellows. There were about half a dozen of us, young leftists desperate to travel, seeking adventure and an opportunity to change the world. It was for this reason that the director of the program explained the following:

> Many of you are going to arrive at your destinations and ask yourself, "Why am I teaching English? Why, here in the midst of poverty and desperation, am I teaching something of so little practical value? Why am I not building houses or plowing fields?" The answer is that wherever you go, there will be people already who know how to build houses and plow fields. They can do it better than you, and more cheaply. All that you have to offer these people at this stage in life is your fluency in English.

I was, of course, devastated to hear this. Perhaps I was most annoyed by the fact that I knew it to be true. I never wanted to admit to myself that I wanted to be a hero, and I wanted to admit even less that I would not get the chance to be one.

However, this did not stop me from trying. I taught English for one academic year, during which time I hosted an independent creative writing workshop out of my house for the students I felt had the most promise. I wanted to give ten students and myself the chance to hash out ideas in writing outside the confines of a classroom and curriculum. It was one of the most rewarding experiences of my life. We discussed sex and drugs. We argued about Marx and capitalism. We also talked about our hopes and dreams and all the barriers that stood in our way. It was through this that I finally came to understand the tragedy of the Chinese countryside: People who had fought for decades to build their own lives and be proud of who they were had been told by generations of leaders that they had to wait their turn. After five decades of waiting, these college students had no hope of being proud, they wanted only to escape and leave the ruins of development to someone else. I felt that the director of the fellowship program had been only partially right. While fluency in English was the only skill I had to offer, for these students it was as big as building a house or plowing a field. I was giving them the opportunity to do what they wanted—to leave the countryside behind—whether I agreed with them or not.

I left in May of 2005 to conduct research for Human Rights Watch on rural peasants who were bringing complaints of local corruption to the central government. Every peasant we spoke with was warned in advance that speaking to Human Rights Watch carried a serious risk of political retribution. However, no matter how much we warned, every person we spoke to looked me in the eye and begged me to help them. They begged me to get them justice for a relative killed, a sister raped or a house torn down by local officials. All I could do was look back at them and know that, at best, I would write a report that would receive international attention and probably get this person thrown in jail. No matter how careful I was, I knew that at least one person I spoke to would be worse off for having helped me. I could not stop asking myself what on earth I was doing all of this for. I was pushing for change on a system-wide level, but what could I do to help *these* people?

In May of 2006 I traveled to Jordan with the National Labor Committee. I was interviewing Chinese and Bangladeshi workers who had flown to Jordan looking for a job, only to have their passports confiscated by their bosses on arrival. They were then told that if they left the factory compound they would be arrested by Jordanian police for not having a legal work visa. The factory management was then able to force workers to work for a fraction of the legal minimum wage. Some workers were not paid at all. Many were raped or beaten. Again, these workers looked at me and asked me for help. They needed their back wages to support their relatives back home. They were willing to stay in Jordan and sew clothing for L.L. Bean and Wal-Mart, but they wanted their passports back. Again, all I could tell them was that I would write a report, call some newspapers and sit in on meetings at the U.S. State Department to see what would happen. In the end, many of the workers received their passports back. Many factories began to pay workers regularly and operate under a regular 40-hour work week.

In China, I helped write a report about abuses against real people. The result was that some people were hurt and jailed, and the system did not change. It was simply not in the interests of the central Chinese government to help these people. In Jordan, I helped write a report about abuses against real people. The result was that most people got at least some of what they wanted. It was in the interest of Jordan, under the U.S.-Jordan Free Trade Agreement, to help these people. However, I am under no illusions about what will happen a month from now or a year from now, when I am no longer in Jordan and the *New York Times* is no longer writing articles about the situation.

After all that I have been through and all the many jobs I have held trying to help people, I still don't believe that the only real skill I can offer anyone in need of assistance is my fluency in English and Mandarin. I have more to offer. A legal education from [target law school] would be a significant step forward. I want to understand the real results of legal reform in China. I want to understand what force international law has when it comes to helping workers. I want to acquire the skills necessary to help those that ask for my assistance. The next time a person looks me in the eye and asks me for help, I want to do better than writing a report and hoping that someone is in the mood to listen.

JDMISSION REVIEW

Overall Lesson

Even an amazing story will not be great unless you tell it well.

First Impression

I appreciate the candidate's straightforwardness and how she moves briskly into the action without a long, wordy introduction.

Strengths

Every once in a while, a concerned law school candidate will say to me, "But I haven't spent years abroad helping sweatshirt workers fight for their rights." This is precisely the type of essay such applicants wish they had the experience to write. This candidate has an abundance of intriguing experience, which provides the basis for a potentially impressive essay.

However, what makes this essay so strong is actually *not* its substance, regardless of how powerful and troubling that substance is, but rather the candidate's writing—how she presents her experiences and, most importantly, shares how they affected her.

What a fantastic line this is: "I never wanted to admit to myself that I wanted to be a hero, and I wanted to admit even less that I would not get the chance to be one."

Because this sentence is so powerful, the long quote preceding it is fine, but typically, you should not include such a lengthy quote in your personal statement.

From this point on, as I move through the essay, I am right with her. I am with her as she questions the validity of what her program director told her, and I am with her when she describes her work for Human Rights Watch and ends the paragraph with three powerful and tragic sentences:

> No matter how careful I was, I knew that at least one person I spoke to would be worse off for having helped me. I could not stop asking myself what on earth I was doing all of this for. I was pushing for change on a system-wide level, but what could I do to help *these* people?

Weaknesses

In the penultimate paragraph, the candidate offers a very interesting contrast between her experiences in China and in Jordan:

> In China, I helped write a report about abuses against real people. The result was that some people were hurt and jailed, and the system did not change. It was simply not in the interests of the central Chinese government to help these people. In Jordan, I helped write a report about abuses against real people. The result was that most people got at least some of what they wanted.

The candidate begins by making an interesting and high-stakes distinction here, but then she fails to tell us what she thinks about this disparity—and this is a significant omission. She misses an opportunity for reflection and leaps straight into her "why I want to go to law school" paragraph.

Final Assessment

I would recommend that the candidate keep most of this personal statement as is, but I would encourage her to seize the opportunity at the end of the essay to reflect more on the differences between her experiences in Jordan and in China. She is clearly very thoughtful and intelligent; the earlier lines of her essay (which gave me chills) proved this to me. So I know she has the ability to make her final paragraphs sing. She just needs to do it!

PERSONAL STATEMENT 20

Start long, not short.

The emphasis the Chinese government has placed on reforming the legal system appears to be a step towards democracy and political progress. It is easy to hope that a reformed legal system will provide a framework in which citizens can demand their rights. However, one must ask oneself why a one-party state would allow this to happen.

I have worked with rural protesters who have given their lives in a vain pursuit of justice. Chinese workers have lost their pensions, their limbs and their livelihoods and now wait patiently in court rooms and labor bureaus for the law to make them whole again. These men and women I have met do not contest the government. They do not contest an economic system that favors the few over the many. Under a one-party state in which a handful of men decide the fates of many, people do not question the justice of the laws themselves.

Legal reform will not transform the power structure. It will not lead to democracy. Reform must be targeted at helping those that can be helped, but it cannot be the end of the struggle, and reformers in the West who want this to happen must not allow the pursuit of a better legal system to blind them to the greater changes that must be made.

NOTE

This essay is the "Yale 250," the short essay required by Yale Law School in addition to the longer, standard personal statement. The candidate who wrote this Yale 250 essay also wrote the essay in personal statement review #19. Because she, as many applicants do, linked the two essays, this Yale 250 submission will be reviewed in light of the candidate's longer personal statement.

JdMission Review

Overall Lesson

Do not settle for an overly simplistic or less than fully developed thesis for your Yale 250 essay; start by being ambitious in your writing, and then cut later, if necessary.

First Impression

The candidate's first paragraph confuses me—I have to read the last sentence twice to figure out what she means by "this." I determine she means "a framework in which citizens can demand their rights," and I thereby deduce that she is suggesting that the one-party state of China is unlikely to become a democracy even though the government has said it will reform its legal system. I believe she could explain her point more clearly.

Strengths

In this essay, the candidate successfully takes the personal experiences she presented in her longer personal statement (#19) and extrapolates from them a thesis on China's legal system as a whole. This tactic works for many Yale applicants—keeping the primary personal statement more personal and then using the 250-word essay to philosophize on an idea or ideas introduced in that personal statement. But this candidate's personal statement is better written than her Yale 250 essay. Her personal statement is coherent, seamless, and easily readable, whereas this essay is somewhat clunky, academic, and, in places, hard for me to understand.

Weaknesses

What does the candidate intend the link to be between the second and third paragraphs? In the second paragraph, we are introduced to people who do not "contest" the government. In the third, we are told that reform will not be enough. I do not see a direct link between these two points. I am sure the candidate has one in mind, but she needs to express it more clearly.

In addition, I feel that her "reform is not enough" thesis is a bit sparse. I know from reading her other essay that she has a wealth of experience working with rural peasants, and through those situations, she has developed an equally rich stash of opinions based on what she observed in others and in herself. For that reason, I suspect she can go further than merely saying that reform may not be sufficient. What *are* the greater changes that must be made? I have a feeling they are related to the people she discusses in paragraph two—possibly convincing them to challenge the government. But I do not know, and consequently, I cannot draw any hard conclusions about her points.

Final Assessment

I would encourage this candidate to clarify precisely what she wants to say about the reformation of the Chinese legal system, and I would push her to be more ambitious about conveying her true message within the allotted word limit. I recognize that the 250-word limit is extremely restrictive, but I also know that with judicious phrasing and substantial collaborative cutting, candidates can successfully say *quite* a bit, even in such a small amount of space. (This is true of all word limits, by the way.)

PERSONAL STATEMENT 21

Write about more than motherhood.

So many essays, so little time. That is how it often feels as a mother trying her very best to guide her youngest daughter through the never-ending college application process. I certainly felt quite like that the first time around, with my eldest daughter, Sophie. And when it was her younger sister Camille's turn, I experienced even more exhaustion as the catalogs piled up in our mailbox, then on our front porch once it began to overflow. But this time I had a new reason to feel tired, a reason that I'd kept hidden as a secret even from my very own family. That reason was that I was planning my own return to school, as well.

I remember the moment I decided to do this as if it were yesterday. It was almost exactly one year ago, last spring, and Camille had received her very first promotional packet from a college that she was quite interested in. As I poured over the idyllic photographs of rolling hills of flowers and smiling young student faces, contemplating the next step in my daughter's long journey to adulthood, I realized that a new leaf was being turned over for me, as well. This would be the very first time in all of twenty years that I'd have an entire empty nest all to my own self (except for our beloved Cockapoo, of course, but, as a dog, he hardly counts.) My husband works somewhat long hours as hedge fund manager. Suddenly my Etsy shop selling hand-beaded necklaces and earrings, the very one that had been so fulfilling in recent years, especially whenever I had rare long stretches of time to myself, just didn't seem like enough to fill up my longer, lonelier days in a big house all by myself.

I immediately remembered a dream I'd put aside so many years ago. I'd felt in the past that it was a long shot, to put it mildly, just a daydream to pass the time and escape into a different life, if only temporarily. But suddenly, like lightning, it did not seem so farfetched, silly or impossible. After all, had I not spent the past twenty years doing just about twenty different jobs, all of them 24/7? Being a mom is the equivalent of being a small business owner, a psychologist, a construction worker, a carpenter, an artist, a nurse, a chef, a tutor, a seamstress, an accountant, a coach, a personal shopper and stylist, a mediator and countless other professional titles. The thing was, I'd managed to master them all out of necessity, because that is what moms do.

As rewarding as my career as a homemaker has been, and I cannot think of a richer way to have spent the past two decades of my lifetime, the truth is that my motivation was always about the needs of my husband, or my children, or, to be completely honest, even my dog. All of my family took precedence over my own needs and desires, and especially dreams. I turned the thick, shiny page of that beautiful catalog, and they came flooding back.

Being a mom and watching both my daughters grow from dots on a sonogram picture into rambunctious youths, and finally, beautiful and mature young women, going on to be accepted into some of the most prestigious schools in the country has made me realize that I truly can conquer any feat that I set my mind to accomplishing. I am confident that I can add one more career to that list, especially when, for the first time, I am doing it for myself. It is time to take my own dream off hold, to turn off the countless legal dramas I have enjoyed on television, and to take part in the real thing. I have no doubt that the skills I have gained in my twenty years of homemaking will prove themselves invaluable when applied to the rigorous and rewarding field of law. I look forward to showing everyone just what moms are made of.

jdMission Review

Overall Lesson

Moms, writing about being a mother is fine, but do not write *only* about being a mother.

First Impression

I think this candidate succeeds in making the most of her first paragraph. She introduces herself, her essay topic, and the conflict she will discuss.

Strengths

The candidate's arc—meaning the progression and development of the essay—is strong, and she does a reasonably good job of writing about having been a stay-at-home mother for the past 20 years. She also does not apologize for choosing to stay home to raise her children, which I think is a good approach. You never want to seem as though you are apologizing for something in your personal statement, be it your GPA, your LSAT score, or your background.

Weaknesses

I think writing about being a stay-at-home mother is completely acceptable in a personal statement, though I know some JD admissions consultants might disagree with me. I tend to believe that if you are writing about *you* and what has really happened and/or what matters to you, you can make it work in an essay. I do not think this candidate needs to go back to school before she applies to law school just to have something to write about, nor does she need to dig into her memory to write about a college experience from 25 years ago. Again, I know others would disagree, but I have personally worked with several candidates in their 50s who wrote about being mothers and were accepted into their desired programs.

But here is the difference: this candidate needs to explain *why* being a mother has prepared her for law school and/or sparked her interest in the law. For example, did she have to fight in some way for her children's rights in their school system? Did she encounter any educational policy issues? Did her daughter's college textbooks inspire her? What about law attracts her, and how does that relate to her experience of motherhood? We need some information along these lines.

I also find myself wondering whether this essay is more of an addendum explaining the candidate's lack of formal work history. I do not mean to say or imply that she has *not* been working, of course; I am referring rather to the employment "gap" in her professional resume. For the essay to lose this quality, the applicant needs to more successfully draw a connection between her past experiences as a mother and her current interest in pursuing a law degree.

Another minor point she should address is the awkwardness and excessive informality of some of her statements and phrases, such as "The thing was..." and "I realized that a new leaf was being turned over for me, as well." This sentence in particular contains both a cliché and a passive-voice interpretation of that cliché, and it simply does not read well.

Final Assessment

I would advise this candidate to do some brainstorming—perhaps via some stream-of-consciousness writing—about why she wants to attend law school, and *Law & Order* is not allowed to be on her list of reasons (or any other TV shows). Is her role as a mother truly related to these reasons? If so, great—she can begin her revisions there. If not, she should consider whether motherhood really is the best angle for her essay and explore some other possibilities that might work better.

PERSONAL STATEMENT 22

Expand your scope beyond your childhood.

My parents got divorced when I was in pre-kindergarten, and then my father got divorced again when I was in second grade. My mother went through her second divorce when I was a freshman in college, at the same time as my dad was going through his third. Both of them are in new relationships now (with people whom my brother and I call their future ex-husband and ex-wife, respectively). So you could say I have a pretty solid understanding of divorce.

Perhaps it is for this reason that I did what I did my freshman year of high school.

There was this girl Jane who, truthfully, was pretty unintelligent—when she spoke, her observations fell just short of the mark. No one really liked her, and Jane was often the entertainment, the one to tease, the one at whom we could laugh because she never seemed to understand that we were laughing at her. I wouldn't call us bullies, because I don't believe Jane ever felt she was bullied. I believe she saw us as her friends.

Jane lived next door to my good friend Mary, who told me one day that Jane's parents were in the middle of a messy divorce—a topic about which I, of course, knew quite a lot. One afternoon, Jane's parents had had an enormous blow out on the driveway in front of the house one day. She heard them screaming and Jane's mom was crying.

The next day, Jane didn't show up at school. Then she missed several more days in a row. When she finally came back, she cut the last three periods and then skipped three more days. This went on for several weeks before Jane and her parents were called in to meet with the school's administration.

Later that day she stayed in school but she was even more quiet than usual. When I asked her if she was okay, she told me that she was pretty sure she was going to be expelled. I asked her where she was going everyday and she replied, "I walk to school, but then sometimes I just keep walking."

I asked her if together we could go to the vice principal, Mr. Wagner, because I had a few things to say on Jane's behalf. She agreed and we went to the administration wing. Mr. Wagner saw us right away. I told him that Jane was in the middle of an incredibly difficult time. I told him that she was practically raising her little brother and herself since her parents were so distracted. Jane cried which backed up my story up. Pretty soon I could tell Mr. Wagner was on our side. He promised he'd talk to the rest of the administration. Sure enough, the next day Jane told me they were going to let her stay.

The next year Jane left our school because she and her mother moved. But I always felt so good about meeting with Mr. Wagner and confidently pleading Jane's case. It made me feel like it was my calling—speaking for those who could not speak for themselves.

It runs in my blood, I think. My aunt is a lawyer and so is my father and my grandmother. There are a lot of Janes in the world who need their side supported by someone with a strong voice. I will do everything in my power to use my voice to speak for those whose voices aren't quite as strong. It is a gift I look forward to using, if you will give me the chance to use it.

JdMission Review

Overall Lesson

If you write about your childhood in your personal statement, you must find a way to tie it to your adulthood.

First Impression

I am hooked by the first paragraph—the candidate's story rings true, is a bit heartbreaking, and is concisely written. The language is well suited to the content.

Strengths

The climax of the story is good. She speaks to the vice principal on Jane's behalf. The candidate's story choice is also good, because it involves a clear connection to law and advocacy.

Weaknesses

The beginning of the third paragraph—"There was this girl Jane who, truthfully, was pretty unintelligent—when she spoke, her observations fell just short of the mark"—is, quite simply, unacceptable. Although this essay does a pretty good job of conveying the candidate's capacity for empathy, this sentence is problematic not only because the arrogance is unbecoming, but also her choice to include this remark suggests a lacking in her critical thinking ability. The candidate must offer a more nuanced description of Jane, and if she cannot, she should refrain from describing Jane at all.

The candidate should eliminate the following sentence for the same reason—it likewise comes across as callous and manipulative—"Jane cried which backed up my story up." Until I read that line, I had had no inkling that she might have been embellishing her story about Jane's situation.

Finally, claiming to be from a family of lawyers tends to be effective only if you use the fact to make a more interesting point than just that you should probably be one, too. The candidate could use the end of the essay to delve more deeply into what she believes and wants professionally as the adult she is *now*. She could return to the topic of her parents' multiple divorces or perhaps discuss certain ideas about the law and justice that she has learned in school—something to incorporate more of who she is today into the essay's conclusion, which is currently based entirely on something that happened to her eight years earlier.

Final Assessment

I believe this essay could be richer and deeper in places and sound more intelligent overall. The candidate has the bones of something here, but as is, this essay will not get her accepted into any great schools. Without additional analysis and a more nuanced discussion of what she believes being an advocate means, the essay actually makes the candidate sound a little immature. I found myself forgetting that she is a college graduate. To effectively convince the admissions committee that she is ready for law school and capable of being a lawyer, she needs to show that she is prepared for what lies ahead.

PERSONAL STATEMENT 23

Do not suggest that you
need to change.

My father was wrongly convicted of first-degree murder when I was four years old. It sounds dramatic, I know, but it is the foundational trauma that would forever alter the course of my life, leading me through the darkness of despair to the light of the law in my quest to make sense of personal tragedy.

As a young man growing up without a paternal figure, I found myself falling into many of the traps that have claimed countless others from broken homes. There was little supervision or overt guidance in my family. My older sister left home at sixteen, when I was but twelve, and my mother was preoccupied with enormous tasks—namely making ends meet while fighting her own depression and soldiering on with my father's defense despite her meager economic resources. The latter seemed an especially losing battle—appeals were promised but either never materialized or led nowhere. Lawyers either made promises they couldn't deliver or refused to represent my father despite a friend-of-a-friend-of-an-ex-coworker's-uncle assuring my mother that "*this was the one*" who could rectify injustice, and *pro bono* at that.

Once I hit adolescence, I was done losing this war and sought only escape of an ironically self-destructive kind. Whether chugging the beers we had procured from older siblings or pitying adults outside the 7/11, committing acts of petty theft and artless vandalism, or engaging in increasingly dangerous "dares" that left us gasping with exhilaration after cheating death or dismemberment, it was clear that my friends and I were up to no good.

Despite my nascent nihilism and flirtations with self-destruction, I managed to maintain good grades in school. School was another escape of sorts, and I found comfort in delving deep into abstract subjects that seemed to have nothing to do with my damaged life. I excelled at advanced math, chemistry and molecular biology and the most arcane aspects of American history. Because of this, I was able to obtain a full scholarship to SUNY-Purchase, which I attended for lack of anything better to do.

Two more events occurred in the spring of my freshman year that would forever change the course of my life: my father committed suicide in prison and I transferred out of Classical Liberalism and into Intro to Criminal Law. The former led to the latter. I cannot adequately describe the decimating despair, nor the guilt-inducing tinge of sweet relief that the war was over, even if we had lost, and my family could finally rest. After her own suicide attempt, my mother went into treatment and began to put the pieces of her life together. My sister returned to help. I felt the need to do something, anything to contribute to my family's healing and, perhaps misguidedly, chose to abandon my path of academic escape and instead confront my fears. It was one of the best decisions I ever made.

I became hooked on the law and its powers of salvation, at least for future clients and myself, if not for my own father. In his memory, I swore that I would do everything I could to make sure our justice system works for everyone, regardless of social status, income, or any of the other factors that unfortunately relegate some to a lower tier of representation. Whether I will be a public defender, working within an NGO or in private practice taking on ample pro bono cases, I do not know, but my passion for equal justice under the law is the clearest part of my life. I want desperately to acquire the tools and position needed to help the most vulnerable, and have dedicated myself completely to this task. I need to do my best to right the wrongs of our beautiful, if imperfect legal system. After years of avoidance of the real world, I need to take responsibility and grow into the man I want to be, a lawyer who would make my father proud.

jdMission Review

Overall Lesson

Your theme should not be that you *need* to change.

First Impression

Wow. Okay…I am with you.

Strengths

The writing is quite good in places. I particularly love the phrase "my nascent nihilism and flirtations with self-destruction." The applicant is knowledgeable enough to use uncommon words correctly, which is—unfortunately for society but fortunately for him—rare.

Weaknesses

The candidate's syntax is occasionally off, by which I mean forced or confusing. For example, the sentence "My older sister had left home at sixteen, when I was but twelve" would read more naturally without the "but." He should simply say, "My older sister left home at sixteen, when I was twelve."

And I found this sentence confusing: "Whether chugging the beers we had procured from older siblings or pitying adults outside the 7/11, committing acts of petty theft and artless vandalism…." I was originally unsure whether he was pitying the adults or the adults were pitying him. I now realize he means the latter, but the sentence structure suggests the former. (To correct this, he could add "from" before "pitying adults.")

Finally, although I think his "old self versus new self" theme can work, it will only work if the shift has already taken place—not if it is taking place *as he is writing*. Suggesting that attending law school is a prerequisite to a critical perspective shift , as he does in his last sentence, is too precarious: "After years of avoidance of the real world, *I need to take responsibility and grow* into the man I want to be, a lawyer who would make my father proud." In this instance, the applicant is basically selling himself on the promise that he *will* change.

What if someone said to you on a first date, "Listen, I'm a mess. I am really not a great person, but I'm ready to change." Would you want to date that person?

The good news is that this candidate does not have to lie. He *has* already changed. He changed when he decided to alter his trajectory. And judging by how he writes and what he shares, he is in many ways *already* the person he says he wants to become. His issue is a stylistic matter, not a personal one.

Final Assessment

This essay is very close to being excellent. With a little language cleanup and some trimming and revising wherever he suggests he still avoids responsibility, this statement can become a powerful piece of his application.

PERSONAL STATEMENT 24

Ensure your topic has appropriate breadth.

"Opening up" doesn't come organically to everyone. The truth is, most of us have a very hard time finding a way to de-clog and allow oxygen to flow freely throughout our bodies. There are of course tools, but they are not always so easy to find. Sometimes you come across important tips in magazines or on television: They might be breathing exercises to help with circulation, or workouts to get your blood flowing, or even drugs to open up the blood vessels in your lungs as wide as they can open.

Being open is the first step one can take in becoming a whole and complete person. For me the first time I felt truly opened up, occurred thanks to something fairly simple. I had always had a stuffy nose. I don't know if I was living with low-grade allergies or some kind of nasal irritation, but for the most part, I breathed in and out of my mouth if I needed to take in full breaths of air.

It wasn't the best way to live life, and certainly not the most attractive. Let's face it, "mouth breather" is not necessarily how a person wants to be thought of. But I didn't have much choice considering there was no fast and hard diagnosis and not much in the way of treatments, although I tried changing my diet and on occasion, resorted to nasal sprays.

One day a close friend brought over a small plastic blue tea pot-like contraption and with a smile pronounced it a "neti pot." I had never heard of one before. It turns out a neti pot is actually the oldest form of something called "nasal irrigation" whereby the nose is cleansed of toxins and debris with nothing but warm water and iodized salt. The word "neti" itself comes from the Sanskrit for "nasal cleansing." The practice comes out of the Ayurvedic yoga practices of India and can be traced all the way back to ancient yogis — male yoga masters — as one of the six cleansing practices called "kriyas." The belief was held that the neti pot would functionally clear and strengthen breath, purify the nose and lead to deeper and more effective meditative practices.

I have to admit, I was skeptical. But at my friend's prodding, I filled the pot with about a cup of warm water — what one might use for a comfortable bath, then mixed in a quarter teaspoon of iodized salt. Once the solution was sufficiently stirred, I placed the arm of the pot, per my friend's instruction, and leaned my head over to the side above the sink.

At first the results were unremarkable. As I slowly poured the water into my nostril, it immediately poured back out again. I stopped and implored my friend, frustrated that the front of my shirt was now splashed with salt water. My nose and sinuses were so blocked, there was simply no way for the water to pass through them. But my friend remained steadfast. She told me that I had to keep pouring until the blood vessels softened and the mucus could loosen up. Not wanting to disappoint my friend, I tried again. Again the water simply ran down my cheek, but I finished a complete pot nonetheless. Then I refilled the pot and poured it into my other nostril. This attempt too, simply filled my nostril and then retracted back out again and down my other cheek.

By the time I had a filled a fourth pot with the solution, I was ready for my friend to leave. She promised me that this could be my last try, now that the front of my shirt was soaked as well as the front of my jeans.

This time, the strangest sensation overcame me as the water entered my nostril then seemed to stream across my nasal pathway, looping generously into my other nostril and then out in a rivulet that splashed delicately back into the basin. I almost wanted to sneeze, as the water tickled its way around my nose. Immediately, I filled a fifth pot and ran the water through my nose the other way. It felt so good, my friend had to tell me to stop so that I wouldn't irritate my delicate nasal passageway.

I let the air flow into my nose, down my throat and into my lungs. It was revitalizing and wonderful. For me, the neti pot was the greatest tool I have ever found, and it represents my philosophy, which is to open up to life. Ever since I adopted this philosophy, my life has become full, open and flowing. It has made me profoundly ready to move forward in my life and career. As an aspiring lawyer, being open has lead me down the path toward law school. With every breath I find myself closer and more deeply enmeshed in my dreams.

Who knew that something as basic as a neti pot could change my life? But after that day, I traded in my friend's plastic version for an authentic ceramic pot. I made my practice more of a ritual that would represent a cleansing three times a day. Today my momentum is clear, directed, and most of all fluid.

jdMission Review

Overall Lesson

If you are a strong writer, you have no excuse for picking a weak topic.

First Impression

The introduction is a bit cliché and uninteresting, but I like how the candidate shares a true story from her life early in the essay. In addition, the transition from a metaphorical "opening up" to a literal one is logical—though the subject matter is a bit unpleasant.

Strengths

The candidate's writing is quite good. She is able to share a personal narrative and hold the reader's attention—a surprisingly difficult task for many applicants, and a vitally important one, given that the school's admissions reader has probably reviewed 100 other essays since breakfast. Moreover, that she is able to capture and maintain the reader's attention with such a trivial—and sometimes unpalatable—story is a testament to her writing ability.

Weaknesses

I have to question how seriously the applicant is taking the essay, which is a problem. Did she choose this topic because the neti pot really did change her life, and if so, what does that say about her? Perhaps she has been very fortunate if the worst thing that has ever happened to her—as the essay seems to imply—is a stuffy nose. Not that she needs to write about the worst tragedy of her life, but if she is going to choose such a low-stakes and, frankly, slightly gross story to convey who she is, she must do a better job of linking her original "opening up" metaphor to her views, beliefs, and dreams—as well as to her law school aspirations.

She ends her essay with the following: "I made my practice more of a ritual that would represent a cleansing three times a day. Today my momentum is clear, directed, and most of all fluid."

This summary statement sounds trite and uninspired, and it lacks a critical, intelligent application of her discovery. The candidate could instead take her essay in one of several different directions. For example, she could discuss the importance of ritual. Or she could detail more specifically how her life has changed since discovering the neti pot—not just literally, but also what being more "open" means in actual practice.

Finally, she needs to find a smoother way of connecting this change in her life with her current aspirations to attend law school. As is, the transition does not work.

Final Assessment

I would advise the candidate to set this essay aside and return to the basics. Thoroughly brainstorming other possible topics could benefit her tremendously. She has the writing skills necessary to deliver a powerful essay, and better topics than the neti pot discovery may be buried in her personal history. However, if she wants to move forward with this theme, she will need to edit her personal statement with a heavy hand, searching in particular for overuse of the expression "opening up" and taking care not to assume that her readers will naturally understand what that means. She must instead elaborate on real-life examples of the metaphor in practice.

Personal Statement 25

Avoid implying that law school
is your last resort.

You might be wondering what a guy like me is doing even applying to law school. After all, I spent the last twenty years of my life criss-crossing the highways and byways of these United States in a beat-up van, playing rock 'n roll music to drunk people in bars—the seedier, the better. You might think that I am the type of guy that would need the assistance of a lawyer, not the other way around. But the fact of the matter is that it was that very beat up van, on that very winding road, leaving yet another seedy bar, that was the location in which I first realized something very important.

Allow me to set the scene: I was quickly driving along the Pacific Coast Highway about two years ago, on a beautiful summer's night. My band and I had just played The Bucket outside of sunny San Francisco, and were going to LA where we could crash out before playing at a club called The Smell. "This is the life," I thought to myself sincerely on that beautiful night as I drove. It was one of my favorite drives, but nonetheless, I found myself distracted. Events had transpired that had made me unable to just kick back and drive smoothly and calmly through the dark night. This was because I was feeling angry. Very angry, in point of fact.

When I first graduated from Berklee College of Music, it was the 1990s. The 90s might as well be a different planet from today, so far as the music industry is concerned. Things were not generally fair to musicians, but there was a lot more money floating around to throw at them. Many musicians would find themselves suddenly on major labels with serious contracts, making expensive music videos and having their album distributed all over the country, even internationally. Nevertheless, most of these bands would leave the roller coaster ride with no money to show for it, but at least they had a good time. You cannot put a price tag on the stories we have.

Unfortunately, that joyride would come to an end soon after I graduated and became a professional musician, so I didn't get to enjoy the perks for very long. Soon, I was just another guitar player trying to make ends meet, except now there were a hundred other guys just like me, and not enough money to go around. However, dreams aren't rational, so we all kept scrambling for the crumbs of the shrinking pie. This led to many of us signing on to contracts that were just completely unfair.

Unsurprisingly, that was the reason why I was so angry on that highway. My friend Tony's band had just headlined the show my band and myself had played back in the day. Tony is a bit younger than me, however he is a very accomplished player and songwriter. The audience went crazy for him, and his band should have been about to break big. But the thing that I knew, the thing that the audience did not know, was that they were stuck in a bad contract. All the heartbreaking tales of loneliness that had just practically brought tears to all their eyes were tied up in an album that their label had made clear they had no intention to release. The reasons were both stupid and typical, wrong beats per minute for radio, too depressing, no single. Nonetheless, they played their hearts out to the crowd, making them love these new songs that they would decidedly never be able to purchase. The situation was inspiring to me. However, it was also unfair.

I thought of my own circumstance: yes, I loved music more than anything in the entire universe. I loved listening to it, I loved playing it, I even loved driving in a busted van all night in order to be able to do so. But I was barely breaking even. had no savings, despite wanting to start a family with my girlfriend for years. The sad fact was that the music industry was ruining music for me, ruining the thing that I most loved.

It was then that I had a thought, which became an obsession, which is still burning within me as I type these words. To save the thing that saved my life I needed to make it a labor of love, not commerce. Music should be something I do because I want to, not because I need to be on the road forty-five weeks out of the year just to keep myself fed. Instead, as a profession, I would look to the law. I would become a lawyer so I could make certain that guys like Tony didn't sign such terrible contracts and protect my fellow musicians forever more. And, with that inspiration, hopefully I have perhaps finally found a professional home.

JDMISSION REVIEW

Overall Lesson

Never resort to "X did not work out, so law is the next best choice."

First Impression

The applicant needs to ditch the entire first paragraph. One should never, ever begin an application essay by apologizing for oneself or by telling the admissions reader what he/she is thinking.

Strengths

The candidate's writing is vivid and compelling. His descriptions of scenes enable me to visualize them, and I like what I see. He is a good storyteller, and that can be a useful quality for a lawyer.

The arc of his essay can also work. The candidate is hoping to become a lawyer because after witnessing firsthand the legal challenges musicians face, he wants to help them. But the essay needs substantial revision.

Weaknesses

The applicant occasionally uses high-brow language that seems unnatural for him and ends up sounding awkward (e.g., "in point of fact," "events had transpired," "the location in which"). Although I actually like his conversational style, the essay needs fine-tuning in places where the tone becomes slightly *too* conversational (e.g., "crash out," "You cannot put a price tag on the stories we have").

He also needs to eliminate the implication that he is pursuing a legal career because he has become disillusioned with music. "Law by default" is never a good angle for a prospective law student—and it can be a somewhat dangerous one at that. The difference between the message he is sending in his current essay and the one I think he is actually trying to make is small but significant: because the music industry has been disillusioning for him, he wants to pursue law so he can help make the industry better for other artists.

Finally, for a similar reason, his last sentence does not work. It is too passive and implies that he is applying to law school because he has no idea what else to do.

Final Assessment

The first fix is simple: he should begin with "I was driving along the Pacific Coast Highway...." He can still share how he spent the past 20 years in the music business, but those details do not belong in the opening paragraph. He (perhaps with someone else's help) also needs to make the essay's tone slightly more formal and less chatty. Finally, he must remove the suggestion that he is applying to law school because he is struggling to figure out what comes next in his life (and/or wants a mortgage).

PERSONAL STATEMENT 26

Steer clear of presenting a storybook
version of yourself.

I can't believe it has taken me fifteen years to admit that what I felt was love when it presented itself as agony. I suppose that's what time and age teach you. But I was six years old, and my Aunt Linda, a serious fitness buff, took me to the gym for the first time. It was across the giant avenue with an island of trees pouring down its middle from the strip mall with my favorite greasy pizza joint.

The first day was all about fearlessness and flying across the balance beam like I was on flat ground. My strong arms were a solid match for my light body—small on the scale by which we measure children. The second week was the same.

I didn't hear the grown ups talking, but one day my Aunt Linda and my mother sat me down in our kitchen and told me that I was better at gymnastics than any of the other girls. I had never really thought about it.

My Aunt Linda said, "You have the most balance and grace."

I nodded, and then went back to drinking my chocolate milk.

"Do you want to take more gymnastics?" my mother asked.

I smiled a big chocolate smile and said, "Yes!"

"Do you love gymnastics?" my Aunt Linda prodded.

I repeated "yes!" because it was true. I didn't realize how those two yeses would eventually transform my life. But one thing was certain: there'd be no more chocolate milk or greasy pizza for a long, long time.

Every day I began waking up at five AM to meet my Aunt on the driveway. I'd climb into her car and spend three hours at the gym. Afterwards I would go to school, having already missed the first part of the day where everyone sings the national anthem and the teacher takes attendance by calling out something from your list of favorites from the beginning of the year in lieu of your name. I never got to hear "Ariel from the Little Mermaid" for my favorite singer, or "Hamburgers with Pickles" for my favorite dinner called out so that I could respond, "Here!"

Instead I tumbled and twirled, balanced and jumped. My body became stronger and harder for my arms to toss around. So I had to lift weights. My muscles ached. I never got enough sleep. Waking up became a chore and a battle my mother and my Aunt Linda always won. I went to tournaments and competitions, championships and exhibitions.

When I was nine, I went to my very first national competition. My hair was bound up in a bun, tightly wound so that no stray strand could escape. I thought I looked beautiful and grown up. My Aunt Linda put a little red lipstick on my cheeks and lips. I leapt across the balance beam like it was the earth. I tumbled across the floor exercises like I was made of rubber. I flew around the uneven bars like a bird. And when I landed, arms held high above my head, the audience cheered and I felt happiness—pure and explosive.

I won that day. And when I got home, I made myself the first chocolate milk I had had since I was six. My mother and my Aunt Linda smiled at me.

I turned to them and said simply, "I'm done with gymnastics."

They nodded. They knew.

Nine years later, at my high school graduation my Aunt Linda gave me a gift. When I pulled apart the wrapping paper I saw my gold medal framed with a photograph of me, age 9.

It reminded me why I lived for gymnastics for three years. Because I had worked so hard at something once, I had become one of the greatest at it, in my age group, in the world. But then I had gone back to being a kid when it was time to leave it behind.

It's in that spirit that I am dreaming of becoming a lawyer. I believe that when you do something you should do it with fearlessness and passion. But it must be tempered by a commitment to living life and staying true to your own heart. Much of law seems like it is about making money or winning trials. But for me, it's about discovering the truth and mastering it, like each individual exercise in the world of a gymnast.

I had no regrets when I left gymnastics. But every once in a while, when the sun is warm and the grass is green, I'll run across a brick wall like it's part of the earth, I'll bounce across the lawn like I'm made of rubber, and I'll swing from an available set of monkey bars like I'm a bird. And when I land, arms held high above my head, I'll feel happiness—pure and explosive.

JDMISSION REVIEW

Overall Lesson

Do not write about a storybook version of yourself.

First Impression

I am intrigued—this essay has a strong beginning. I want to know more about the candidate and am not distracted by the confusing writing in the final sentence of the first paragraph ("island of trees pouring down its middle"), which needs revising.

Strengths

This essay is, fundamentally, readable, which is rare. It has a clear arc—she tells the story of her gymnastics career from beginning to end—and includes a pivotal moment of change. She smoothly relates what she learned from gymnastics to her decision to attend law school. I like her statement "It's in that spirit that I am dreaming of becoming a lawyer." It captures the abstract but nonetheless believable link between two seemingly very different pursuits, gymnastics and law.

Weaknesses

The candidate resorts to clichés and cute language that ultimately weaken her essay—for example, "I smiled a big chocolate smile and said, 'Yes!'" I point out this habit so often that discussing it again makes me feel like a broken record, but perhaps that highlights precisely why repeating this critique is so important.

This is going to sound harsh, but bear with me: describing how cute you were as a kid is a bit like inviting people to look through 500 of your vacation pictures. You cannot imagine they would *not* be fascinated by what you have to share, but the truth is, they are not.

The candidate's "chocolate milk smile" may have been adorable to her aunt, but the admissions officer at Harvard does not care how cute she was. Likewise, the sentence "Instead I tumbled and twirled, balanced and jumped" sounds almost as though she is writing a children's story about a gymnast.

The urge to write as though you are describing someone other than yourself is understandable—writing about yourself is intimidating, and doing it well is extremely difficult. The personal statement might be one of very few times in your life that you are ever required to do so. A natural impulse is to emulate the way others have written about your chosen subject, so if you are writing about childhood, you might naturally be tempted to use "cutesy" language.

Do your utmost to resist that temptation.

What should this candidate do? Describe the way the bars felt under her fingers or the way the pad felt when she landed on it. Describe a moment of fear. Describe the hunger she felt, going without her beloved pizza and chocolate milk for so long. Describe these in the voice of the adult she is now, and I will want to know her and understand her. In turn, I will be more likely to admit her to my law school.

Final Assessment

I would first have this candidate complete several writing exercises to improve the essay's basic content. I would then ask her to do some free writing to explore her memories and pull out more vivid descriptions of her gymnastics years. Once she has richer, more "adult sounding" material to use, she will need to incorporate that to strengthen the ending, which smartly recalls an earlier portion of the essay.

PERSONAL STATEMENT 27

Skip the Robert Frost quote.

When two roads diverge in a wood, one must choose a path, as the famous poem states, and that choice will make all the difference. On the road of life, paths will diverge more than once. One notable occasion on which I found myself at a fork in the road was when I was applying to college. I find myself at yet another fork now.

Should I go on to pursue another degree in business? Or should I go out into the "real world" and get a full-time job? These questions spun around in my head all the time as I began to wind down my work on my business major. But I spotted another road, one less travelled by: maybe I should pursue a law degree instead.

I may seem like an unlikely candidate for law school because of my final GPA, as well as the fact that it took me six years to complete a four-year program. I arrived at a 2.1 after a series of forks in the road of my life that led me to this unlikely number. As my records will show, I enjoyed an "A" average throughout both high school and middle school. Excelling at school always came easily to me, and I enjoyed learning new things and the sense of achievement. I continued to excel in college, until situations in my personal life caused me to become distracted from my studies, and eventually take a leave of absence. You see, my parents got divorced while I was still in school. This was an incredible shock, they had always seemed so happy and perfect together. We did not see this coming, and it took a terrible toll on my entire family.

For my own part, I found myself unable to concentrate fully on school work as both of my parents, my sister, my brother and assorted other relatives were calling me frequently, often crying or making other emotional demands. I am not resentful towards any of them for leaning on me so hard, as we are a family and that is what we do for one another, even, or especially when a part of us has been broken. At one point my sister even decided to go travel around Italy rather than go to college, upon graduating from high school. For awhile we didn't even know exactly where she was, or who the "friends" she was with were, but eventually we got an address: a villa on the water in a town I'd never even heard of. It was a nerve-wracking time, and I had to withdraw from my own studies to go follow her and stay with her to make sure she was okay.

Once I returned to the United States from six months taking care of my little sister in Europe, I also had to frequently visit, stay with and care for both of my parents, who were going through divorce-related depression. There were many obligations of theirs that I had to take on as my own responsibilities because they weren't doing well enough to take care of them themselves. It was a very difficult and trying stretch of road for me, one on which I learned a lot about choosing direction moving forward in my life.

I am glad to say that with the support of their family, both of my parents have largely recovered from depression. My sister is happily in college, studying literature and getting good grades. I was eventually able to return to school and complete my degree despite the difficulty of returning to school after such a long absence, especially under difficult circumstances, and am very proud of this achievement. All of us have taken different, winding roads that have been determined by the different choices we have made at each fork. I myself have realized that the right path for me leads to law school.

JDMISSION REVIEW

Overall Lesson

"Two roads diverged in a yellow wood"—but not in this essay!

First Impression

Please do not quote or allude to Robert Frost's "The Road Not Taken" in your personal statement. Yes, his diverging roads metaphor is powerful, which is why so many people have already used it, and why you should not, under any circumstances.

Strengths

The candidate is clearly a devoted sister and daughter, and she has the evidence to prove it—significant stretches of caretaking, all around. She might be able to incorporate elements of her supportive role in her family when she rewrites this essay from scratch.

Weaknesses

Let us examine the essay more closely:

"I may seem like an unlikely candidate for law school because of my final GPA, as well as the fact that it took me six years to complete a four-year program."

Do not mention your low GPA in your personal statement—save it for an addendum! Your personal statement is where you *sell* yourself by highlighting what is great and unique and promising about you, not where you highlight your weaknesses as an applicant.

"I arrived at a 2.1 after a series of forks in the road of my life that led me to this unlikely number."

And if your GPA is that low, do not draw attention to it by mentioning it *again*.

"As my records will show, I enjoyed an 'A' average throughout both high school and middle school."

Unfortunately, those As will not help you now, because admissions officers do not see your high school and middle school records, nor do they care about them.

The candidate goes on to write what should be an addendum essay explaining her low GPA. Again, this content does not belong in her personal statement.

Finally, her essay ends with a meandering reflection on her family, which reads more like a diary entry or a letter to a close friend than a law school application essay. Why does she want to pursue a legal career? We have no clue.

Final Assessment

After removing the clichés and the Robert Frost allusion (and misquote), the candidate should repurpose this as an addendum essay to her application and start writing a new personal statement from scratch. As I mentioned earlier in this review, she could possibly use some of the same material; her devotion to her family could certainly be the basis for a strong essay. In this current essay, however, the candidate does not discuss that devotion in a way that lends itself to a solid personal statement.

Personal Statement 28

If you drop a bomb, see it through.

When I first studied the law, I knew it was love. I was sixteen, a budding feminist, and increasingly angry about the sexist discrimination and harassment that were part of my daily life, both in and out of school. Every girl I knew had stories of gender-specific, unfair treatment and abuse, yet when we brought our complaints to authority figures, they were generally dismissed. My own mother was sometimes sympathetic but never had solutions. As often as not, she would explain with exasperation that life was just not always fair, and things were much better for girls in the aughts than when she was growing up. I felt that despite my voice, I was not heard. Despite my Herculean efforts, I felt powerless.

Then everything changed. It was junior year and I had the opportunity to take a class in Constitutional law. It was within those formerly oppressive walls that I came to see how the law could function as an equalizer. The law provides a structure in which words must be heard. Speech within the law was empowered, unlike my futile attempts as a measly individual at school or in my community. Those working within the law have institutional power, power they lend by extension to those disempowered and silenced, through representation. While the promises of equality held in the Constitution have yet to be fully realized, they are the finest standard I have ever encountered, a goal towards which to strive.

In high school I signed up for every law-related class I could, even starting an extracurricular "law club" where interested students could further study. I applied for an after-school job as a courier at the law firm of one of my parents' friends, just so I could regularly visit the courthouse and legal libraries, and pick the brains of the lawyers who amiably tolerated my surely distracting inquisitiveness. That summer, I was accepted into a month-long intensive research internship at the District Attorney's office. Those weeks were among the most enthralling I had ever spent, and they stoked the flames of my encompassing passion.

After being admitted to New York University, my first order of business was securing an internship with the Center for Constitutional Rights, an organization I admired for its focus on social justice issues. CCR litigates class action lawsuits that have the potential to further civil and human rights. There

I saw the Constitution truly at play as a "living document," a guiding beacon yet open to interpretation, with the potential to liberate and help us achieve a more genuinely just society. I finally felt that my high school dreams were being realized as I helped CCR harness the power of the law to effectively fight for the rights of the underdog.

Within the New York City social justice landscape, I began meeting activists who made me question my goal of making change through the legal system. I saw valid suits lost or, perhaps worse, won, but the victory was circumvented by loopholes that left us no better than when we started. I began working with various community-based groups focused on grassroots organizing, wondering if more on-the-ground action was what we needed. Many of my friends were early participants in the Occupy Wall Street movement, and I spent more than a few exciting nights in Zucotti Park myself. For a moment it felt like nonviolent revolution was at hand, and had nothing to do with me passing the bar.

Of course, Zucotti was cleared and many of my friends were arrested. Some spent years fighting unfair charges. This again made me see the clear necessity of social justice-oriented lawyers. I saw that however romantic the idea of sudden revolution, lasting change comes in often maddeningly small increments, and that the good fight will inevitably continue long after I'm gone.

I apply to law school with the maturity and patience earned by exploring many paths to justice, all of which have brought me back to the urgency and art of the law. My adventures have only deepened my ultimate commitment to the legal process, and the Constitution remains my most-cherished poem.

JDMISSION REVIEW

Overall Lesson

Do not drop bombs and then change the subject.

First Impression

The first paragraph is not bad, but the candidate uses the phrase "sexist discrimination and harassment" and then moves on without elaborating, as if those terms need no further explanation. Particularly because she characterizes this treatment as a daily occurrence for her and all her friends, she needs to describe what happened. The situation sounds quite extreme (and horrible, if true), so she must provide some concrete examples to support her claim.

Strengths

Overall, the candidate tells a smart and persuasive story about her journey to law school—her conversion to belief in the power of law, followed by disillusionment, followed finally by a rediscovery of its power, albeit with newfound wisdom. Her writing is clear, her sentences are well structured, and she comes across as intelligent, academically oriented, and thoughtful.

Weaknesses

The weakest link in this essay is the beginning—the worst place to showcase a weakness. You should avoid introducing provocative, hot-topic terms without explaining what you mean by them, particularly when you do not revisit the subject(s) later in the essay. (We never find out what kind of discrimination and harassment the candidate and her friends endured.)

In addition, the paragraph about the Center for Constitutional Rights (CCR) is missing something. The candidate describes her time there as transformative, but she uses language so abstract that even after reading the whole paragraph, I still do not know what kind of work she did there.

Finally, while her chosen topic works, I am not sure it is her best one. I am left wondering whether fleshing out the incidents described in the first paragraph would better support her thesis than offering a painstaking overview of her law-related activities over the years.

Final Assessment

Fortunately, the essay has some room for expansion, because it is shorter than the standard two to four pages. I would advise the candidate to rework the first paragraph to include more specific details about her high school years, expanding it to two paragraphs or more if necessary. She also should revise the CCR paragraph, adding concrete evidence to illustrate why her experience there was so meaningful—or, if the revised first half of the essay reads as more compelling than the second, she could cut this section altogether.

PERSONAL STATEMENT 29

Stay away from superficial themes.

My brand is something I have honed intricately over many years, in fact for as long as I can remember. My parents work in advertising—my mother as a graphic artist, and my father as a web developer—have taught me to think in terms of "my brand." This education has been both one of extrapolation as well as one of observation. My parents consider everything they do publicly as an extension of their brand as individuals and also as a married couple, and then finally as members of our family. Even privately, from the way they raised my brother and I, to the way they interact with each other within their marriage, everything is juxtaposed against their consideration of their every action on an aesthetic level.

I appreciate that such behaviors ring of falsehoods and Mad Men-esque superficialities. But the truth is, approaching the world with an eye turned from the outside in, I believe has improved us as individuals and as the "[Last name] Family." For example, my brother Thomas, who is the youngest in the family, five years younger than me and adopted at the age of two from Malawi, has been grilled since he could talk about how he wishes to be perceived. I was given a similar treatment throughout my youth. Since I was seven when Thomas joined the family, I witnessed first hand my parents helping him to mold his brand. It has been nothing short of a masterclass in branding taught by two of the world's true branding masters.

Thomas is now nineteen and in his second year at Harvard University. He has always said that he wants to be an American man of color who could over-come a childhood of little to build himself an adulthood of plenty. He dresses like a man who cares about his perception in the world. He behaves like a man worthy. We are all very proud to associate him with our brand.

It is this desire to create a semblance of worth and even greatness in terms of those we love that has helped us all to remain our best selves.

In college it took me until the middle of sophomore year to lock down the appropriate friend group. They were attractive but unaffiliated, put together but smart, kind but focused. Later, I realized that my choice, although cerebral and part of a larger "plan," also meshed perfectly with the needs of my heart.

A mindful and deliberate approach to living is what a branded life entails. Choices are generated, not immediately from the heart, but with a sincerity of the mind that places the results of the choices above the choice itself. My life, from my own perspective, and hopefully the perspective of the world, is one of which I am supremely proud. I believe I will improve the brand of your great law school. I will be a student and one-day alumnus of which you will make a point of associating. You might think that this is a shallow way to consider me, but it is certainly truthful. I will be the kind of lawyer and woman about whom your school will be happy to say, "[applicant's name]? Oh she went here. And boy are we glad she did."

jdMission Review

Overall Lesson

Do not settle for a shallow theme.

First Impression

I am unimpressed off the bat. "Branding" oneself the way she does sounds far too much like "being fake." If this is the topic of her essay, which I expect it to be, it feels superficial and uninteresting.

Strengths

Not much here is working, but these two sentences present an opportunity to use her subject in a productive way: "I appreciate that such behaviors ring of falsehoods and Mad Men-esque superficialities. But the truth is, approaching the world with an eye turned from the outside in, I believe has improved us as individuals and as the '[Last name] Family.'" Nonetheless, she does not seize that opportunity.

Weaknesses

The applicant's theme feels thin to me, and I finish reading the essay without learning anything about her except her view on branding—on which she has pontificated for two pages. She argues that thinking of oneself as a "brand" is a good thing, but we do not actually know *how* she thinks about herself or what her particular brand is, or how it has "improved her as an individual" as she claims. We hear a little about her brother and her parents. However, all we know about *her* is that she found some friends in college based, in part, on their appearance—which is, to be frank, a little concerning.

If the applicant wants to keep the theme of "branding," she needs to *talk* less about what branding means and its importance and focus more on *showing* us what her own "brand" is. She would also benefit greatly from discussing why she is interested in attending law school and what her plans are for her career after she graduates.

Final Assessment

This essay needs to reveal more about the candidate. She should make that goal the starting point for her revisions. Then, she should reassess whether the branding theme still works. If she imbues enough of herself into the essay, she may be able to remove the discussion of branding altogether.

PERSONAL STATEMENT 30

Remember your reader is
not your therapist.

After my divorce, I didn't want to get out of bed. My seven-year-old son Sean, however, expected me to, so I did. I have to admit, he has been my saving grace. I am very lucky to have him, because not only does he get me up in the morning, but he makes my day actually feel worthwhile. There is no less cliché way to say that. My son is my greatest and only reason for getting up each day.

But I began to realize, over time, that my husband was not coming back. He met a young girl after the divorce that he proposed to last month. She looks a lot like I did in 1982 when we met. I think he needs to relive something. Maybe he'll do it all better this time around, with less sullen silences and shutting people out. I wish this for him. And of course I wish it for Sean.

When we got divorced I was truly the most alone I have ever been. My ex would take Sean for a week here, a weekend there, and suddenly the house grew into an enormous castle. But there was only emptiness. The walls were like bubbles holding all this air but zero oxygen. And I felt so completely unable to breathe. I wondered what Sean was doing. I called him about three times a day, but I wanted to call him about sixty.

What was all of this doing to my son? I couldn't imagine. Sean would cry when he would leave me. But I don't think he actually wanted to stay with me. I mean, who would? I was so interested in every move he was making. I was always calling out to him, so that he would run over and find me. And then I would make him hug me or sometimes lay next to me in bed, even though the sun was out and he wanted to play.

All this went on for about a year and half. By this time my ex was dating a lot of different women. Our mutual friends couldn't look me in the eyes to tell me how great he was doing when I'd ask how he was. They'd shrug. But I saw his online profile and I heard from Sean that he was dating. My ex was happy. Happier. I tried not to let this destroy me.

Instead of dying, I decided to add some things to my life. The next time my ex took Sean, I decided to visit a nearby town and look around. It was late spring and I began going to flea markets and garage sales. I started buying old beautiful items, cleaning them and posting them online to sell. Soon I had made some money and was able to trade in my car for an SUV in which I could transport a fair amount of stuff.

I cried while I drove. But I also started to think a little bit about my future. I decided it was important that I do everything in my power to become a version of myself of whom I could be proud. More importantly I needed to become someone of whom Sean would be proud. This broken shell of an ex-wife and ex-person wasn't going to impress anyone, and it was going to kill me. I remembered how a young version of me, before I became a wife, had wanted to go to law school. She had wanted to help people and understand the rules of our great nation.

Right now, it's a big change from where I was two years ago, but it's a positive change. I feel very lucky. And so does Sean.

jdMission Review

Overall Lesson

Getting personal in your personal statement is certainly okay, but remember that the admissions reader is not your therapist.

First Impression

So many conflicting impressions make up my first impression! Although I love the first and second sentences of the initial paragraph, the next three venture a little *too* far into save-it-for-your-therapist territory. Furthermore, rather than advancing the story she is telling, they simply belabor the idea she has already introduced. I find the candidate's use of the present tense in the last sentence of the first paragraph concerning—is her son *still* the only reason she gets out of bed each day? If so, maybe she is not ready for law school…

Strengths

The candidate comes across as utterly truthful—the whole piece is heartbreak-ingly sincere. Her decision to pursue a law degree seems like a good one, and I find myself rooting for her. That said, based on *this* draft of her essay, I probably would not admit her to my law school.

Weaknesses

Much of the first five paragraphs definitely goes too deep into therapy territory. The admissions committee does not need to know so many emotional details about the difficult breakup of her marriage. While I am very sympathetic to-ward what she has experienced, she needs to heavily edit the entire first half of her essay (or find someone else to do so), for both substance and grammar.

For example, consider the following passage: "He met a young girl after the divorce that he proposed to last month. She looks a lot like I did in 1982 when we met. I think he needs to relive something. Maybe he'll do it all better this time around, with less sullen silences and shutting people out. I wish this for him. And of course I wish it for Sean."

After evaluating the relevance of this particular fact at all, if she determines that it advances her essay and supports her thesis, here is how an improved version might read: "He met a young girl after the divorce and proposed to her to last month. Maybe he will succeed this time around—of course, I wish that for Sean."

And so on.

Finally, the candidate dedicates the vast majority of her essay to discussing the person she does *not* want to be—that is, the person she *used* to be. Instead, she should focus more heavily on the "new" her, which means she must augment the section in which she remembers and recommits to her interest in law school. What triggered her to think about law school again in the first place? What were her thoughts and feelings as she contemplated the idea? How has her decision to pursue a JD affected her relationships and/or her world view? What does she hope to do after graduating with a law degree? She needs to address these questions to properly balance her essay.

Final Assessment

In addition to revising the first paragraph as described in this review, she needs to rid the subsequent section of its excessive detail to streamline and shorten the description of her difficult period. Finally, she should bolster the hopeful third section of the essay, in which she describes her increasing independence and ambition. Without these changes, I would not advise her to submit this personal statement to any school.

PERSONAL STATEMENT 31

Take care not to bury your lede.

When I was a child, the lurking fear of public speaking hid behind every classroom, every ceremonious event, and every solemn funeral. It was a monster that lay in wait for me, patiently ready to pounce— and pounce it did, viciously and often. By high school, I was determined to overcome this obstacle through scrupulous preparation. I engaged in debates only after studying both sides of an argument. I memorized quips and some learned semantic tricks. If asked about free trade, I could recite chapter and verse of both sides. If asked about the Iraq war, I could stand on either the Democratic or Republican platform. Whenever I could defeat my opponent with a clever twist of words, I felt victorious, as if I had unhorsed my competitor in a verbal joust. And so I continued to speak and to hone my oratory skills—until the words of yesterday compelled me to reevaluate my motivation to speak today.

Ronald Reagan consoled the hearts of the country with, "We will never forget them, nor the last time we saw them, this morning, as they prepared for their journey and waved good-bye and 'slipped the surly bonds of earth' to 'touch the face of God.'" John F. Kennedy reinvigorated the spirit of selflessness with, "Ask not what your country can do for you, ask what you can do for your country." These were more than words; they were the clarion calls of rhetorical genius that inspired the world. Ashamed of the empty rhetoric in my arsenal and challenged by their wisdom, I decided to search for my purpose to speak. In college, I took on rigorous courses on a gamut of topics ranging from East Asian cultures to the ethics of international law. I pursued public sector work in nonprofit and took on internships related to community service. I searched for ways to not only hone the power of speech, but also to develop a voice that would inspire others.

By the end of my time at Columbia University, I was certain about what I wanted to speak for upon graduation. I wanted to return to my ethnic homeland, and do work related to conflict resolution. I took the job at Border Peace School (BPS) located near the Demilitarized Zone (DMZ) in South Korea in order to learn on the field about the DMZ and North-South relations. I was confident in taking the job because of my undergraduate coursework, past work experiences and linguistic fluency. It was not until my first phone call at my new job that I was challenged once again.

My assignment for the day entailed calling the military branches along the DMZ in order to discuss entry into the Controlled Civilian Zone for our summer peace walk program. The conversation started smoothly enough. My tone was composed and confident, but as the conversation progressed, I froze in self-conscious silence. It was as if I reverted to my childhood self, entirely lost for the words to speak. I managed to hee-haw my way through questions and explanations, but I was not prepared to understand the officer's military jargon. After a confused conversation, he warmly asked, "excuse me, but are you a gyo-po?" He wanted to know if I was a Korean who immigrated to a different country. I chuckled in confession, trying to mask the humiliation, but inside I felt naked; in a matter of minutes he revealed my inadequacies for the job.

I quickly realized that my rhetoric and knowledge accrued throughout college was of little use in the new country. I had to start from scratch again. I worked on my professional Korean with the help of generous coworkers; although many of them could speak English, I insisted on conversing in Korean to improve at a rapid rate. I took initiative to take on the role of giving tours to BPS visitors in both languages to learn more about the organization and practice my translating skills. In spite of my novice initial attempt, I was resilient in staying in contact with the military and eventually gained access for our peace walk. At times it was embarrassing and frustrating fumbling on my words, but I am proud that I had taken on a challenge to perfect a new language in an unfamiliar country. By working with people with not only a different language, but also a different culture, I needed to help them see from my perspective and also see from theirs. In Korea it was no longer just about how to speak, but also how to make the other person understand.

By the end of job, I was able to implement several DMZ related programs under a project proposal of 50,000,000 Korean won (around $50,000), which our team received through government funding. Because of the small staff, I took on more responsibilities than I had expected taking the job, but that challenge just propelled me to work harder. The greatest personal success, however, was that the same military officer who I spoke to over the phone served as our guide during the peace walk. I shared about my experience and also listened to his while trekking along the 155-mile border. Though he was guiding us to monitor our activities, the fact that a military officer walked side by side with activists was a symbolic victory. It was a hopeful step toward peaceful reunification.

Through this time, I discovered that language and understanding each other's narrative is the most important part about reconciliation. Going forward, I want to learn critically about alternative dispute resolution in the legal field. It is important to me that as a lawyer, I can engage every alternative solution before going into litigation. All these are examples of what I hope is in the future for negotiating a peaceful reconciliation between two Koreas. Although it is a lofty dream, my hope is that in the future I could play a small role in the mediation between the two countries. I believe that my interest and experience in the field of mediation, peace and conflict reconciliation and interest in Korea will allow me to be a unique and valuable addition to [the target school's] Law Program and particularly its unique Center on International Conflict and Negotiation will be an ideal place to apply these past experiences and pursue my legal studies. Gain the skills needed to assess, analyze disputes and resolve them efficiently and creatively.

In Korea, I learned that the key to communication is not simply about articulating my views clearly and winning debates, but also about recognizing commonalities, working on differences, expressing our weaknesses and understanding. In high school I learned how to speak, and in college I found what to speak for, and now I am ready to truly communicate.

JDMISSION REVIEW

Overall Lesson

Do not say you discovered a purpose or learned something important without actually saying what that thing is.

First Impression

I like that the candidate begins her essay by discussing her fear of public speaking. I also like that she describes how she would argue both sides of an issue to practice—an interesting mention that reveals much about her.

Strengths

From the candidate's fear of public speaking, to her finding a reason to speak, to her revising that purpose after arriving in the field, this essay has a solid theme. The candidate has a strong voice, and her reflective nature is clear. The essay includes a great deal of compelling material—too much, in fact. It needs to be shortened. That said, the essay has a powerful beginning, middle, and end, which should somewhat facilitate the candidate's revision process.

Weaknesses

Although referencing historical people and events can be a useful tool, I do not understand how the particular quotes the candidate highlights in this essay fit into her narrative. Was *what* these historical figures said the compelling factor or *how* they said it? Was the feeling behind their chosen words what influenced her or the emphasis the speakers gave those words? How do these quotes illustrate the link between the candidate's life of arguing both sides and finding her "purpose to speak"? The two quotes she has chosen are very different and were spoken by two very different presidents.

At the climax of her essay, the candidate writes, "I needed to help them see from my perspective and also see from theirs. In Korea it was no longer just about how to speak, but also how to make the other person understand." Understand what? She does not say what she wanted to convey—what *was* her purpose for speaking? The candidate simply needs to add a short phrase or sentence to state what she wished to communicate. Her mention of the project proposal is likewise missing key information. I am impressed that she played such a significant role on a project of that scale, but what exactly *was* the project? Finally, in the last two paragraphs of the essay, she mentions the importance of people understanding each other, but this section would have more impact and make more sense if she were to clarify what she hoped to communicate when she first arrived in Korea.

Final Assessment

This essay needs more substance yet fewer words—a tricky combination. The candidate should add the missing elements I have noted in this review, but she also needs to go through the entire essay with a fine-tooth comb to eliminate excess verbiage. For example, the essay begins with these two sentences: "When I was a child, the lurking fear of public speaking hid behind every classroom, every ceremonious event, and every solemn funeral. It was a monster that lay in wait for me, patiently ready to pounce—and pounce it did, viciously and often." Here, she should delete the second sentence, because its only role is to elaborate on the first. By making similar edits throughout the essay, she should be able to create enough space to add the necessary additional material.

PERSONAL STATEMENT 32

Make no apologies for yourself.

"Why would a visual artist apply to law school, and why should we possibly take him seriously?" may be the first and second questions that spring to your mind upon seeing my application. Well, firstly, allow me to address your initial question, which will hopefully allow you to draw your own conclusions as to the second. I can do this best by sharing a simple and common story, the tale of how a boy became a man.

Ever since I was old enough to sit up by myself, I have been fascinated by comic books. Before I could sit up, in fact—my mother has told me that my first favorite item of clothing was a Superman insignia onesie, and that I would weep when she took it off. Once I could express my own preferences, though, everything became crystal clear: I was into comics. Superhero comics, to be more précis—each week I would spend all of my meager allowance at the comic book shop, catching up with all my Marvel and DC friends, friends whose regular acts of selflessness, cunning, and bravery would become a lifelong source of inspiration. Batman and Spiderman were my favorites, of course. These characters provided me with a powerful ethical blueprint with which to navigate the morally complex universes we each call home.

It was only a matter of time before I would realize what you surely have already noticed: since I could not escape to Gotham within the real world, perhaps I could be a part of the world that created it. I had always been a creative child, perhaps too creative, some would say, as I often spent my classroom time sketching while day dreaming about fantastical situations rather than concentrating on social studies. But I learned to put my imagination to good use as I developed my artistic skills, eventually being accepted to Parson's School of Design. I majored in graphic design, a discipline which relieved my parents a bit, as it was nearly practical. I could indulge my visual artist side in a manner that had commercial applications.

I had a wonderful time in New York City, and I did not abandon my love of comics throughout my studies. Rather, comics became a regular source of inspiration in my school work and other design. I found myself especially inspired by the iconic New York City landscape, living there really helped bring the urban crime worlds inhabited by my favorite super heroes to life.

As I began thinking about ideas for my senior thesis, I realized that, as much as I thoroughly enjoyed designing websites and book covers, I wished I were majoring in illustration instead. I wished that I could develop a thesis project around the themes of superheroes and superheroism. I began sketching ideas for large illustrations of superheroes and related scenarios, which explored these issues in depth. This sent me into an intense period of thinking and reading about superheroes in general and my relationship to them specifically. I dove into online forums and academic texts. I realized that more so even than creating artistic images of superheroes, I truly wanted to become a superhero myself. I turned back to my childhood heroes as figures of justice and righteousness, and thought seriously about how I could be a person who does that kind of work as well, in the real world. The answer came to me in a burst: be a lawyer. I really could fight crime and stand for justice. I never would have thought back when I was doodling in class that those very same doodles would eventually show me the way to law school, but that is, in fact, the strange path my life has taken. I feel more passionately about the idea of prosecuting possible criminals who each in turn enjoy the right to representation, and watching how true justice plays out, than I have ever felt about another dream in my life.

JdMission Review

Overall Lesson

Avoid bad beginnings and generalities.

First Impression

The candidate should not apologize for his artistic background. Although I *did* wonder why a dedicated artist would apply to law school, he does not need to *tell me* that I was wondering that. He should just explain what draws him to law school. If you assume the admissions committee is out to prove you wrong (which is not true) and frame your argument that way, you will just make your admissions reader uncomfortable—and this might negatively affect your candidacy.

Strengths

In the following well-written portion of the essay, the candidate identifies the ethical sensibility underlying his comic book infatuation:

> Each week I would spend all of my meager allowance at the comic book shop, catching up with all my Marvel and DC friends, friends whose regular acts of selflessness, cunning, and bravery would become a lifelong source of inspiration. ... These characters provided me with a powerful ethical blueprint with which to navigate the morally complex universes we each call home.

He goes on to describe how his affinity for comic books led him into the arts and how his graphic design education led him back to comics, which in turn led him to law. When I write it out this way, his story sounds more convoluted than it does in his essay—he actually takes a story that could easily seem too complex and makes it work. How? His story reads as authentic. I believe him—I believe the reasoning behind the steps he has taken, and I believe he really *does* want to study law.

Weaknesses

The candidate needs to cut the entire first paragraph and begin with "Ever since…."

Also, he should delete certain lines or make them more robust. For example, saying, "I had a wonderful time in New York City" adds nothing to either his argument or his story development. What does the phrase "a wonderful time" mean in this instance? I can guess, but I should not have to. Instead, he should explain that in New York City, he unearthed shapes and structures and modes of expression to which he had not been exposed in Montana. Or he could share that he witnessed crime for the first time—not the comic book kind, but the real kind—and describe how that made him feel.

Finally, I would like him to provide more evidence at the end of the essay to support his decision to become a lawyer. Since he made that decision, what has he done, if anything, to help prepare himself for a law career? Has he secured an internship at a law firm, volunteered at a local legal aid office, or read books on the law? If he really did make a wholehearted decision to pursue law, his actions would likely offer proof.

Final Assessment

I would work with the candidate on enriching his story and strengthening his case for becoming a lawyer, and I would strongly advise cutting the first paragraph. The good news is that the second paragraph actually is a *good* beginning. (Remember this tip: If you feel stuck with a bad beginning, rather than repeatedly trying to rewrite it, imagine how the essay would read if you just took it out and started with the next part.) After he did a little more work on his essay, I would want this candidate at my law school.

PERSONAL STATEMENT 33

Avoid forcing a metaphor that does not apply.

No one can prepare you for the moments that will change your life. For some, these moments might be loud: a major award won to thunderous applause, a touchdown scored to a cheering crowd, or a speech given on a public platform for all the world to hear. For others, these events are quiet: a realization made while jogging, an answer to a nighttime prayer, or even a solution to a problem occurring in a dream. For me, the moment was somewhere in between these extremes.

You see, I was a member of one of the most revered fraternities on my college campus. I was proud of this accomplishment and of the legacy of service to the community that my fraternity was a part of. We did not just drink beer and hit on girls, we believed in community service and helped shape the future. The importance of my fraternity was stated in the very word: *fraternity*, meaning "brotherhood." My fraternity brothers were not only friends or social acquaintances, they were, and are, my family.

Like all families, we would fight. Some of us prioritized legacy brothers over expanding our base. Some of us had anti-authoritarian tendencies that led to conflicts with the university over noise, parties and alcohol, while others of us had a "don't rock the boat" attitude. But none of us were prepared for the conflict that emerged when one of our potential brothers died.

I do not intend to be dramatic by explaining the situation in this manner, but it is the simple truth that a possible future member of my fraternity did pass away during my studies as an undergraduate. He and I had much in common, as well as many differences. I was a sophomore while he was a freshman. I majored in business management while he planned to study accounting. I came to New England from Pittsburgh while he was a native Bostonian. Nevertheless, I found that we also had much by way of common ground in the brief time we spent together at a fraternity social. I found that he was a bright and inquisitive young man with an excellent scholastic record, who was much appreciated by many upstanding citizens of the financial world. He came from a family that delivered on its promises, and I had no doubt that this new student would have been a welcome addition to the fraternity I believed in. I was proud when he chose to pledge, and had the utmost certainty that he would be selected as one of our new brothers.

He did not perish at my fraternity house, he died at another, of alcohol poisoning, during rush. I am proud that my fraternity is not the one that provided this impressionable young man with his fatal shot, but that does not mean that my conscience was clear. As an older brother, could I have provided this mere freshman with guidance that might have altered his path? Did I set the best example I possibly could have? Did I make it clear that he was a strong pledge who did not need to capitulate to peer pressure in order to be seriously considered as a brother?

I do not know the answer to these questions, but I do know that I will think of this possible brother of mine for the rest of my life. This deep contemplation has led me to the conclusion that my next logical career step is one in which I can help guide people onto the correct path and penalize those who have crossed the most just and democratic line that we as a society have imbued with power and meaning: the line of the law. Anyone liable for this tragic loss of promising life must be held accountable.

JdMission Review

Overall Lesson

Do not force a metaphor; if it is not working, lose it.

First Impression

Although the candidate's point is legitimate—a moment that changed his life was neither very "loud" nor very "quiet"—he overuses clichés (e.g., "for all the world to hear") to a distracting degree. In the first paragraph, I want him to focus on making his point and lose the trite language. The same goes for the first two words of the second paragraph: "You see…" No, I do not! Just write what happened.

Strengths

This applicant chose to write about an experience that embodies several key attributes of a successful personal statement topic: it has clear, affecting meaning to him, enough time has passed that he can reflect on it thoughtfully and articulately, and it provides a believable and straightforward link to either who he is now or why he wants to practice law (in this case, both).

Weaknesses

The essay suffers in several places from the same vagueness with which it begins. He writes, "We did not just drink beer and hit on girls, we believed in community service and helped shape the future." However, he provides no actual detail or description of what the fraternity brothers actually did, what kind of community service they provided.

This criticism may sound trivial in the context of an essay about death, but I think avoiding clichés and generalities ("delivered on its promises") by being more specific can strengthen the piece. The more we actually understand about the applicant and this fraternity he loves so much, the more we will understand how the death of his friend affected him.

Next, and more importantly, take another look at his last paragraph:

> I do not know the answer to these questions, but I do know that I will think of this possible brother of mine for the rest of my life. This deep contemplation has led me to the conclusion that my next logical career step is one in which I can help guide people onto the correct path and penalize those who have crossed the most just and democratic line that we as a society have imbued with power and meaning: the line of the law. Anyone liable for this tragic loss of promising life must be held accountable.

I can figure out what he means: he is saying that if anyone committed an act that violated the law and led to his friend's death, that person should be held accountable. And he wants to become someone who holds such responsible parties accountable. But I have to read the text twice to figure this out, and admissions officers do not have time for multiple reads. The applicant would therefore benefit from being more specific here. Who does he think is accountable for the death—the fraternity house that served the alcohol, the liquor store, the university? Or maybe, rather than referring specifically to this instance, he is alluding to similar future situations. He needs to make his focus clear. Does he want to be a prosecutor or a plaintiff's attorney? If he is unsure, he can say so, but he must do so using concrete terms instead of the passive, slightly disorienting statement with which he currently concludes his essay.

Finally, this moment that changed his life does not fit the "loud" versus "quiet" dichotomy he presented in his first paragraph. If I had to categorize it, I would choose "loud," but it does not really strike me as either. It is just a tragic event. The writer needs to either circle back to that metaphor or drop it entirely.

33. Avoid forcing a metaphor that does not apply.

Final Assessment

This candidate should work on the essay's ending a bit more—make it clearer and more concrete. He also needs to remove the clichéd language, particularly at the beginning. Finally, I want him to work on some of the issues in the middle of the essay that I have outlined in the Weaknesses section.

PERSONAL STATEMENT 34

Leave out the wacky gimmicks.

H.E.L.P.I.N.G.: A Personal Statement of Purpose

Ever since I was born, my parents have shared with me the value of help-ing others. Charity, volunteer work, and just plain, old-fashioned lending a hand to your neighbor were all looked upon proudly in my family. In fact, my parents both made helping out into careers: my mother is a third grade teacher and my father is a minister at the First Lutheran Church. He taught me that Jesus was a helper, and that I should be a helper, too. Helping others is the highest service that people can do. Which leads me to a question I have asked ever since I was old enough to ask it: what does it mean to help?

Well, I think I have the answer to that question, and it is right in the word: "helping". H.E.L.P.I.N.G can be easily remembered as standing for: Healing Every Living Person in Incommensurable and New Groups. Let me explain what I mean by this. I mean that it is only helping if we help *everyone*, even people who may be strange to us or seem unimportant. It is not really helping if you only help powerful people because they can give you favors in return, or if you only help people who are your friends or people who are just the same as you. Jesus helped everyone who was in need, and that is how I want to be. That is why, to me, "helping" means "help *every* living person (meaning, well, everyone, from your best friend to a complete stranger, the president or "the peanut gallery") in incommensurable and new groups" (meaning groups that are very different from one another and might be new to you. Social, religious, national or racial groups, not just the groups you are already in or are familiar or comfortable with.)

Not everyone has the same definition of helping. Some people may think it is helping to only help themselves, their family, their church, their team, their school or their town. But when we only help our selves, we leave other people out in the cold. This can make the world unfair.

For example, my high school's soccer team, the Wolves, always had brand new uniforms when we needed them. We often played against underprivileged schools, one in particular, whose uniforms were not always new, pristine or in the most popular style of the time. During my senior year of high school, this other school had a car wash to buy new uniforms, and the coach of our team suggested that we should go to it. But most of the kids enrolled at my school said, "Why should we go help the other team if we want to beat them?" It was a hot day and a lot of kids wanted to be in the air conditioning or spend their money on movies or pizza or other fun activities. The other school did not raise enough funds for new uniforms, and when we played soccer against them, people noticed this. It made my school's team look like rich snobs, even though most of us were not and had our own struggles. Furthermore, we did not win the game. So who were we really helping by not attending the car wash, and sharing our own friendship and good fortune? No one.

At first, I did not understand this. I was just caught up in childish rivalry and was angry that we did not win. It was only after talking to my father about it that I realized I had been a hypocrite. When you don't help "the little guy" or other people who are different from you, you are not really helping at all. In fact, you might really be doing harm. You might be a snob, or even prejudiced. This is an example of why there is so much injustice and unfairness in the world.

In conclusion, after spending my whole life thinking about what it means to help, I am very committed to spending the rest of my life being a helper. And, to me, being a helper in this day and age means being a lawyer. Even if they do not have a lot of money or social prestige, even if they are a part of a discriminated group, everyone has to have a lawyer if they need one. This is one of the fairest parts of the finest justice system on the planet Earth. I hope dearly to become a part of it.

jdMission Review

Overall Lesson

Avoid writing an essay that leaves your reader with the impression that you cannot handle the demands of law school.

First Impression

First and foremost, this candidate needs to lose the heading. I am 100% sure this is a bad idea. Do not use a heading or a title. Ever. You are *not* the exception.

Consider also the very first sentence, which is bad in a relatively standard way: the cliché renders the sentence nonsensical. "Ever since I was born, my parents have shared with me the value of helping others," she writes. Really? Ever since she was *born*, she has been learning the value of helping others? This probably sounds nitpicky, but you should never start your essay with a clearly hyperbolic statement. If this candidate feels she absolutely must begin her personal statement with such a declaration, saying, "Ever since I was a child" would help make the claim a bit more believable.

Strengths

The theme of helping others could work, and the story she chooses to illustrate her theme could potentially be effective with some substantial revision, but it needs to be told in the right way.

Weaknesses

The acronym, on the other hand, does *not* work. It is too gimmicky, and frankly, it also reads quite young—making the candidate seem as though she is of high school age or even younger. This is part of a law school application. The candidate is trying to get into a graduate program for which she will be ex-

253

pected to read and comprehend hundreds of pages of dense text every week, to be prepared to respond spontaneously when cold-called in class, and to sit for several four-hour (or longer) exams each semester. Is she cut out for such a program? This essay not only fails to convince me that she is, it almost convinces me that she is *not*.

The candidate also repeatedly lapses into conversational language that is far too informal for this context. Phrases such as "well..." and "just plain, old-fashioned lending a hand" may be appropriate for an email or text but not for a personal statement essay.

Final Assessment

The candidate needs to completely rewrite this essay, but before she does, I would want to have an honest conversation with her about whether she is truly prepared to handle the rigors of law school. If the answer is yes, she will have to start from scratch on her personal statement. If she opts to retain the theme of "helping others," she will need to make her text *much* more nuanced, incorporate more sophisticated analysis, and clearly apply the theme to her past experiences and her expectations for the future. She can do this by changing the focus of her essay to a later period in life—college, at least, or after college, if she has graduated—and incorporating more sophisticated analysis into her narrative of what it means to "help."

PERSONAL STATEMENT 35

Restrain your ego.

As a talented young person who has succeeded in most realms I have attempted, I am ironically plagued by self-doubt. How can I know my true path? How can any of us? What if I wake up in middle age in a cold sweat, suddenly realizing that I wasted my life pursuing a dream that was not my own? My answer to this quandary came with my introduction to corporate law.

This was a surprising revelation to me. As a child, I had always considered myself a performer first. Drama, chorus, tap, you name it; if I could get up on a stage and give everything I had to an audience, I was fulfilled. I won numerous awards from elementary school through college for my participation in the performing arts. But I had to wonder: was there more? I couldn't shake the feeling that, as enjoyable as I found performance, I might have a higher calling that I just hadn't heard yet. Maybe I didn't think the most I could aspire to as a girl becoming a woman was spangles and a smile. Maybe I wanted to *change the world.*

My parents and friends thought I was crazy when I hesitated regarding where I wanted to matriculate for college. "Julliard, obviously," they said, "or maybe Tisch or Yale School of Drama." Each name sent a shiver of excitement down my spine, but I couldn't shake the feeling that I wanted, nay, *needed* options if I was to truly thrive. My first hint of what these options could be occurred when I lead my high school debate team to victory in the state finals by arguing against school blockage of YouTube on the grounds that it was censorship and also that the website was an important educational resource. At this competition, I realized that formal argument is a satisfying performance as well, and one with wider reaching real-world applications perhaps than singing, dancing, or even acting.

Wanting to explore a more well-rounded education, I was admitted to my mother's Alma Mater: Brown. There I discovered the law. I signed up for "Women and the Law" mostly out of a curiosity regarding feminism, more so than an interest in the law specifically, but once I was in, I was hooked. I saw that the law is what binds all parts of our society together; there is not one part it does not touch. You can't even talk about gender discrimination, for example, without discussing where and how it has been legalized and criminalized. Without lawyers, there would be no title IX, and who is to say that I would have had the opportunity to lead my high school lacrosse team to two championships? Sports are an empowering experience that all girls should have. I realized that as an attractive woman, many expected me to be no more than a pretty face, but it was empowering to show the world that I am more than eye candy. If I want to truly effect change and make the world fairer for women (and men), I need to acquire more power.

It is this idealistic energy that has allowed me to hear my true calling: to be a high-powered and inspiring corporate lawyer who will set precedents by performing on the stage that is the court room, perhaps the most important stage scattered across this great country. The beauty of the legal code surpasses even the most exquisite monologue to me now, and every night I dream of passing the bar and what I will do once I am Leslie Rebecca Murphy, Esquire. I look forward with clear eyes and an open heart to the day when I can use my talents for the greater good, reaffirming the principles that make the United States of America the greatest country in the world, and setting an example for my future daughters.

JDMISSION REVIEW

Overall Lesson

If your first sentence makes you seem unlikable, you will immediately (and possibly irrevocably) lose your reader.

First Impression

Eek. This candidate's opening sentence contains numerous problems. First, one does not "attempt realms." Second, the applicant begins by telling us that she finds her own self-doubt shocking, given how good she is at everything. Forget whether you would want her at your law school—would you even want to *talk* to her for five minutes? Arrogance is extremely unbecoming.

Strengths

The arc of her essay works—she describes her progression from being a performing artist to discovering her greater interest in law. However, her execution is poor.

Weaknesses

The arrogance—which at times borders on ignorance—continues to resurface throughout the essay. Consider, for instance, the statement "I realized that as an attractive woman, many expected me to be no more than a pretty face, but it was empowering to show the world that I am more than eye candy." This statement does not advance her essay and makes her seem privileged in a way of which she is unaware. It reads as entitled.

But her arrogance throughout is actually the lesser problem. The greater one is that she loses me right at the beginning, so I do not care about her enough to notice any of the "good" parts of her essay that follow—the parts that might otherwise move or touch or impress me. I simply want to finish reading her essay so I can get on with my life, because I have already labeled her as annoying. Even as I finish reading, she reminds me that she has made the entire essay about *her*—and not in a meaningful, interesting way, but in a self-conscious, self-involved way. For example, she says, "Every night I dream of passing the bar and what I will do once I am Leslie Rebecca Murphy, Esquire."

Do *not* be this person.

Final Assessment

This essay needs a full-blown rewrite. The applicant could still use parts of it, but she must lose the first paragraph entirely and start with "As a child...." Then she should flesh out her arts background more fully before discussing her introduction to law, which also needs to be meatier. I do not believe this person intends to come across as arrogant—she does not appear to even realize she is doing so—which means she will need help changing the tone of her essay. Although all applicants benefit from assistance with their application essays, this individual especially needs to have someone else (or better yet, several people) carefully review any version before she submits it.

PERSONAL STATEMENT 36

Write an essay no one else
could have written.

It may come as a surprise to anyone reading this that someone like myself thinks I have a shot at going to a law school as prestigious as [the target school]. However, it is exactly people like me who I think would make the best lawyers. I have had to struggle my whole life to learn what it is I want to do—be a lawyer—and thus come to the practice with a greater sense of purpose than many people I know who have wanted to be lawyers ever since seeing their first *Law and Order* episode.

In college, I was determined to spread my wings, and try out as many different disciplines as I could before deciding on a path. Thus, I experimented with a number of different disciplines—psychology, calculus, physics. These experiments, however, were not all successes, as evidenced by my college transcript. However, without the ability to experiment like this, I would never have discovered my true calling, and perhaps would always have wondered whether I shouldn't just have been a therapist or physicist. With these experiences behind me, I can now go to law school with full conviction that this is my true path.

One should not take away from this any misconception about my academic abilities. As you can see, my grades in all law-related fields have been excellent. I received high grades in philosophy, political science, and history. But of course, if I had only ever focused in college on the fields I already knew I would do well in, I would have missed out on the point of a liberal arts education—to expand my base of knowledge. Learning what one is *not* good at is just as important as learning what one *is* good at.

After college, I worked as a paralegal. This gave me a window into the lives of actual lawyers. While I may not have practiced law, I have been to courtrooms and depositions, and have proofread briefs and motions. I have sat in on meetings with clients and engaged in legal writing. That is to say, I have real world, on the ground experience with law.

Law school, unlike many other forms of graduate education, is a professional school. Law school is intended to teach people to go out and practice, not simply to learn theory. As such, it is fitting that my desire to become a lawyer came from my true experience working with legal professionals, rather than simply from pre-law classes or other such class work. Thus, one can be confident that I will not graduate from law school and enter the practice of law only to realize that I enjoyed the theory more than the practice. I know what being a lawyer means, and I know that it is right for me.

People say that most of us in this generation will have three of four careers over our lifetimes. Having dabbled in many different disciplines in college, I am confident that this will not be me. People spend their lives switching from one career to the next in the hopes of finding the right fit for them, losing years of experience in the meantime. Each transition to a new career requires learning new skills and losing old connections. I think that if more students were willing to experiment more in college, they would be better able to settle on a single career that worked for them, as I have done.

I believe that I would be a great asset to [the target school]. My willingness to take risks and experiment, as well as my dedication to the practice of law, will allow me to make a valuable contribution to my law school community.

jdMission Review

Overall Lesson

When people finish reading your essay, they should feel like they know you.

First Impression

Never, ever apologize for yourself in your essay—especially in the first sentence.

Strengths

The candidate presents a couple of ideas that could form the basis of a decent essay, such as learning what she *does not* want to do so as to discover what she *does* want to do and being committed to experimenting and taking risks. However, she does not develop either of them in any satisfying way.

Weaknesses

This essay needs a lot of work. Although it has the potential to be compelling—centering on the candidate's decision to pursue law school after eliminating other options—she fails to convince me that her claims are true. She never shares what she actually likes about the law. Why *does* she want to be a lawyer rather than a physicist? What did she love so much about her "real world, on the ground" legal experience?

I am also not sure what the point of her essay is. She apologizes for herself in the first sentence (which, as I have already noted, is a very bad idea) but then goes on to present all the reasons she is a good candidate.

Finally, she predicts that she will not be someone who changes careers, but by that point in the essay, I know nothing about her that would support her claim. I do not know what she likes about the law or why she enjoyed her paralegal work. I do not know where she grew up, what her family was like, what motivates her, what she cares about, or what she hopes to do with her law degree. By the end of her essay, she is as much of a stranger to me as she was at the beginning.

Final Assessment

This essay demonstrates the importance of having others read and respond to your personal statement before you submit it. To me, it reads like a first or very early draft, yet the candidate strikes me as confident in what she is writing. I find this disconnect concerning, because it shows that the candidate is unaware of how she is truly presenting herself and of the many holes in her argument. This kind of essay could ruin what might be an otherwise strong application. However, the candidate could likely improve it by investing substantially more work, attention, and time on revisions.

PERSONAL STATEMENT 37

Do not rely on big words to sound smart.

My short-term ad hoc career goal is to persevere in buttressing my technical knowledge while studying law. I believe that one needs to possess technical design experience in order to move forward with the development of an appreciable personal aesthetic. Further, I believe that technical design, especially in the realm of architecture, can improve a theoretical understanding of information utilization and generation, which will have an impact on every discipline in the future. A lawyer who possesses the ability to use technical design and architecture tools will be at an advantage, professionally, even if the connection is not immediately obvious.

My long-term objective is therefore to obtain a JD while simultaneously improving my technical know-how and savvy. Ultimately it is my intention to work with architects or technology developers in a legal capacity, as I will have a keen and distinct advantage based on my background, experience and education. I believe this will set me apart and will inspire faith in and respect for my abilities in these fields.

An alternative long-term objective is to obtain my JD in order to achieve greater relevancy in a design or technology position. I believe a profound understanding of the legal system and skills toward its mastery are vital in achieving the heights toward which I intend on advancing.

Both potential paths are not only acceptable to me but they are also titillating.

Through my research, study and acquisition of copious information, I believe I will be able to contribute to the world of architecture and design from a legal standpoint. The reputation of designers and architects might generally be under appreciated by individuals in the legal community. I believe I am equipped with the appropriate tools to bridge this gap, as I feel it also exists for designers and architects in terms of the reputation of the legal community. I believe that law school, paired hand in hand with my own personal study of the technical resources of architecture and design will perfectly allow me to achieve my goals.

[School Name] is of particular interest to me because of the esteemed faculty and diverse student body, as well as the alumni that align themselves with it. I believe that my enrollment at [School Name] will only benefit us both.

Understanding design, architecture and technical tools, illustrates a specific skill set perhaps under appreciated in legal communities. I make this suggestion because the branding, logos and commercials that are most visible to the laymen from firms and law schools indicate that aesthetics are not at the forefront of their interests. However, design, architecture and technology tools and those who are able to master them are important, not just for their ability to make things beautiful, but to illustrate that one is able to conquer other ideas, ideas that are not only presented in words, but are absorbed through the eyes and heart.

My appreciation for and love of these things will make me a better lawyer. They indicate that I am passionate and curious and able to learn other languages that one might not even speak out loud. Law might seem better suited to people with a profound love of words. And while I do love words, I am also passionate about beauty, life and living it to its fullest.

jdMission Review

Overall Lesson

Understand your reasons for applying to law school before you try to convince someone else why you are doing so.

First Impression

Why is this person applying to law school? The entire first paragraph discusses something other than law, though I am not completely sure what.

Strengths

The sole strength of this essay is the applicant's decision to highlight how his architectural background makes him a unique candidate with a potentially desirable set of skills. His attempt to do so, however, falls flat.

Weaknesses

This essay presents a couple of major problems. First, the applicant seems to be using large words to sound intelligent, but his message is unclear. For example, consider the following statements: "An alternative long-term objective is to obtain my JD in order to achieve greater relevancy in a design or technology position. I believe a profound understanding of the legal system and skills toward its mastery are vital in achieving the heights toward which I intend on advancing." After I finish reading them, I do not know what he wants—a career in design or technology that uses legal expertise? What *is* that? Does that even exist?

Second, the reasons he offers for choosing the particular law school are generic and transparently false, and when I reach the end of the essay, I still do not know what he wants to do with a law degree. His essay reads as though he is applying to law school without understanding what a lawyer does—he seems to want to be a graphic designer and have law firms as clients.

Finally, the essay suffers from a clunky, awkward, and repetitive writing style that makes it read as though it was composed for the purpose of SEO (search engine optimization). In addition, some words, such as "titillating," are used inappropriately.

Final Assessment

This essay needs a tremendous amount of work. The applicant must begin by asking himself why he wants to go to law school in the first place. The reason should not be because he wants to act as a communications bridge between architects and lawyers—that is not practicing law and not a good reason to attend law school. If I were working with him, I would ask him to describe to me how he pictures his life as a lawyer. What does he expect to do on a daily basis? What does he *want* to do? Answering these questions is the first step toward crafting a workable essay.

PERSONAL STATEMENT 38

Lose the exclamation points!

I never actually got to be Brutus, at least not on game day. But I was the next best thing. I actually got to spend every game day on the sidelines of Horseshoe Stadium, which was a childhood dream, and I got to make sure that Mike, who played Brutus, had enough water and didn't fall over with the enormous weight of that giant head. (Trust me. On a hot autumn day after two hours, it's hard to keep upright.)

The best part about my job was the promise: If Mike was ever sick, injured, or otherwise unable to play Brutus, I would get to take over. I was chosen mostly because Mike and I were the same size and the other assistant was a girl and the head was so heavy it would make her fall over, which was funny, but also makes for a pretty sad mascot.

The first time I was Mike's assistant, I was really distracted because – wow, the stadium! I had been watching games on TV since I was a little kid with my brother and dad. Actually, the excitement started in the locker room, in the special Brutus area when I helped him get the costume on. Mike was pretty psyched, but I was psyched too, because I was standing next to Brutus! Touching the costume!

So you can imagine how amazing it was the day I got the call. It was the middle of senior year, after Mike and I had been doing this together for about a year and a half. Mike had been in a car accident the night before. He was okay, but the doctor wanted him to sit this one out. So what this meant was that I was going to get to be Brutus. I was going to get to dress head to toe as Brutus on a game day. But it wasn't just any game day. It was the game against our biggest rival. Everyone I knew was there. The crowd was super pumped up and screaming like crazy. You could hear it from inside the locker room practically.

I opened the locker door and put on the red football pants, then the cleats, followed by the famous striped scarlet and grey sweater with the padded shoulders. Finally, John, a new assistant, lifted the head over mine. It smelled a little bit, but when I looked in the mirror, I didn't care. The head muffled all sounds and I felt like I was someone else. I was—I was Brutus.

But just then there was a commotion. I couldn't really tell what was happening. I thought maybe there was a fight in the locker room. Then suddenly the head was pulled off and I looked around. There was Mike. He had decided to come in anyway because he didn't want to miss the big game. I was crushed. I took everything off and gave it back to him. I didn't want anyone to see how disappointed I was, so when they squeezed my shoulder and said, "Sorry man," I just shrugged and smiled.

I brought Mike out that day to cheering that sounded like thunder. The stadium erupted with joy at the sight of Brutus. I stood beside him and pretended that the crushing sound was for me.

JDMISSION REVIEW

Overall Lesson

Lose the exclamation points! (Okay, you can keep *one*.)

First Impression

The candidate's first paragraph works, but just barely. By the end of it, I have concluded that the candidate is talking about being (or not being) a sports team's mascot. Readers familiar with Horseshoe Stadium will understand quickly that he is talking about a university football team's mascot, but those who are not will likely be somewhat confused. For me, he provides just enough information so the suspense is not annoying, but a little more detail would ensure that any reader would feel the same.

Strengths

The essay topic is fun and different, and I love it. And I can guarantee that admissions officers are not inundated with essays about applicants being college mascots, so this candidate's statement would stand out. His story about being the dutiful assistant and nearly playing the coveted role of the mascot ends in sharp disappointment, and he tells it so well that I am genuinely disappointed for him. Moreover, I simply like him.

Weaknesses

This paragraph is confusing:

> The first time I was Mike's assistant, I was really distracted because – wow, the stadium! I had been watching games on TV since I was a little kid with my brother and dad. Actually, the excitement started in the locker room, in the special Brutus area when I helped him get

the costume on. Mike was pretty psyched, but I was psyched too, because I was standing next to Brutus! Touching the costume!

When I read "Actually, the excitement started in the locker room," I do not know if the candidate is talking about his childhood or about the first time he was Mike's assistant. Also, this paragraph has too many exclamation points. Exclamation points are overused in general, and when they pepper a personal statement the way they do here, they can make the candidate sound immature.

Finally, what does this essay tell us about the candidate? Although I find his writing style easy to read and his experience relatable and entertaining, I have no idea why he is applying to law school or why I should admit him. He needs to include some information about his interest in t he law and explain why he believes it is a good path for him. Without these very important points, the essay adds little value to his law school application.

Final Assessment

Because this essay is on the short side, the candidate has room to expand it and share a little more about who he is and what he wants. I want him to use this sweet and entertaining story to reflect on what the experience meant to him and how it shaped him in some way—particularly in relation to his law school aspirations. And although this may sound like a trivial point, it is not: I would also suggest that he remove 80% of the exclamation points.

PERSONAL STATEMENT 39

Correct any imperfect
punctuation.

Crew

"WOMAN OVERBOARD!" My crew career started with a splash. I had been rowing for two weeks and my coach asked me to move from four-seat all the way back to the bow, which entailed climbing over three of my teammates and strapping myself into the seat. I never made it. After keeling over into the river, heaving myself into the launch boat, and enduring the wet ten-block walk back to my dorm, I began reevaluating my extracurricular choices.

Standing at 5'6" and displaying an admittedly stocky build, one could say that crew was not ideally for me. Coupled with the fact that I could barely run a mile without stopping, it seemed that I was ill-equipped for the physical demands of the sport. It didn't help that I had fallen out of the boat within two weeks of joining the team. All in all, I gave the coach, and my fellow teammates, no reason to have confidence in my abilities.

Rather than quit and try my hand at another extracurricular activity, I decided to apply myself to winter training, the indoor season of crew where rows on the water are replaced with sessions on the ergometer, hockey rink stairs, and the track. To say I struggled was an understatement. I became used to bringing up the rear on team runs and finishing last on long distance erg pieces. Gradually however, I noticed a change.

While running or climbing stairs didn't seem to get any easier, I was finishing the same distances faster. Encouraged by my progress, I began to add extra workouts to my weekly schedule. By the time my spring season came around my sophomore year, I had the third fastest 2K score on the team; no one was more surprised than me. But that is where I stayed until I graduated. Having always been a vocal member of the team, I found that my leadership role became more pronounced with my success in training. The team's collective efforts were rewarded senior year, where we finished with a 9-3 season record and were ranked 6th among Division III crews nationally.

At the end-of-season banquet that year, my coach credited me as one of the people who turned the team around and put it on the winning path. "Tara is Tara," he said. "You want her in your boat. She has set the standard for hard work."

My efforts in rowing reflect a "can't quit, won't quit" mentality that I apply to every aspect of my life—my studies, internships, and jobs receive the same dedication, effort, and determination to succeed that I devoted to crew. Furthermore, my participation in a varsity sport has taught me to manage my time effectively and built my stamina in terms of dedicating my time and effort to the task at hand. It is with these qualities that I intend to succeed in law school and go on to work in security.

Crew requires self-discipline, adhering to a set of principles, and holding yourself to a high standard; practicing law demands the same. As a lawyer I will be expected to not only adhere to the law, but also to uphold it, a duty that I am eager to take on. The challenges of law school are daunting, but I welcome them. Freshman year my coach told me I didn't know when to quit, and he was right. My perseverance accounts for a lot of my past successes, and will ensure future ones.

JDMISSION REVIEW

Overall Lesson

Using a lighter tone and topic in your personal statement can be effective, but avoid making trivial mistakes.

First Impression

I am pleased that a female candidate is writing an essay about sports. She comes across as likable and sincere. Also, the candidate's opening is strong, and I remain enchanted throughout the first paragraph.

Strengths

The obstacle she presents seems genuine, and the details she chooses to include provide evidence of her struggle—she falls out of the boat within two weeks of joining the team and finishes last in team runs (some readers may even find these examples endearing). This is a very important point to consider, because when writing an "obstacle" essay, candidates often exaggerate the adversity of a situation to appear brave or resilient. And usually, the fabricated or enhanced challenge will seem implausible—and the admissions reader will see through the tactic.

Because the candidate's change is believable, I admire her and the effort she dedicated to making that change happen. We all understand the difficulty of sticking with something when we are not good at it. When she says in the essay's last paragraph that she will bring this same attitude to her law studies, I trust that she in fact will, because her claim to approach life in this way is believable to me.

Weaknesses

In the penultimate paragraph, she writes, "It is with these qualities that I intend to succeed in law school and go on to work in security." Discussing your longer-term career plans can be good, but in this case, I do not know what type of security she means or in what capacity she intends to work. She does not elaborate, and I have no idea what she is talking about—the Central Intelligence Agency, perhaps, or the National Security Agency? Security at a private corporation? She needs to provide more detail about her plans and goals in this regard.

The candidate also makes a series of very minor errors that all need to be fixed:

- Do not title your personal statement.

- Do not assume that your readers are familiar with specialized terms, such as *four-seat*, *ergometer*, and *erg pieces*—you must define them. Remember that admissions officers work in a different field than you do.

- In general, opt for periods over semicolons.

- Avoid using unconventional spacing or formatting. The version of this personal statement originally submitted to jdMission included some unusual format choices (that we have not recreated here in the book), but this is not a good way to have your essay stand out to the admissions reader. Stick with 11- or 12-point font (ideally, Times New Roman), indent your paragraphs, and do not put an extra line space between them.

- Finally (and this is a very common grammar mistake), do not separate your subject from its verb with a comma. The candidate's otherwise powerful final sentence is marred by being grammatically incorrect. She writes, "My perseverance accounts for a lot of my past successes, and will ensure future ones." "Perseverance" is the subject here, and both "accounts" and "will ensure" are the associated verbs—her perseverance will ensure her future successes—so "perseverance" must not be separated from its actions by a comma.

Final Assessment

This is a good statement—albeit a little on the short side. However, its current brevity means the candidate has room available in which to elaborate on what she means by "security." After she addresses this issue and fixes the minor mistakes I listed in the Weaknesses section, her essay will be stronger.

PERSONAL STATEMENT 40

Recognize that your background
will not speak for itself.

Five years ago, I wrote articles for the local newspapers decrying the mis-education of young Black males. These articles became the basis of the school I founded: [School Name]. After walking the corridors of corporate America and making my way through the public school system, I decided enough was enough. No more talking—it was time to put my thoughts to action, thus [School Name] was born.

Title XI prevented public funding for single-sex education institutions. With very little money, my prospects for creating an all-male urban school were dismal. My options were limited but I was undeterred. I began giving lectures at churches, local bars, barbershops, anywhere I could get an audience to listen to the urgent need to end the destruction of Urban Males. The lectures did generate money, but not nearly enough.

I had to be innovative in order to compensate for the lack of money. I re-organized how the school would operate. [School Name] would operate a like a college, with adjunct professors instead of full-time teachers. The administra-tion and part-time faculty would make up the core of the [school]. The reces-sion made it easy to attract the highly educated professionals to the [school].

[School Name] opened its doors in 2008. My strategy and growth plan were sound. Every instructor had a master's degree, law degree or some other advanced degree. Future plans for a blended learning technique using video conferencing would allow [School Name] to hire some of the best instructors around the world. But my mindset changed, as I witnessed the young men's attitudes and behaviors. The building was often dirty; computers were stolen; and while many of the young men were making academic progress, it was not enough, and certainly not what I anticipated. America had just elected its first African-American president but the students seem oblivious to the election. They stilled called each other nigger.

I knew there would be growing pains, but I did not foresee this one. I had removed all the obstacles that I presumed were what impeded academic achievement for many urban males. We had excellent instructors; there were no unions with which to haggle. There were no subliminal messages of inferi-ority. Yet, here we were still in the same place.

As my thinking changed, so did my conversations. I would often point out to the students how no white people had come to the facility and soiled it—Black people had. No white man stole any computers; Black people did. No white man put a gun to your head and told you that you couldn't read; you made that decision. While years earlier I had stood before crowds discussing the Black man's plight, I was now discussing the Black man's fault.

In short, it became clear to that were cultural issues at play that had not been addressed by the community.

The increased responsibility and unbounded creativity that comes with working for and creating a start-up is unparalleled. Starting from the twin premises that law is a cultural form and that culture carries the regulative force of legal practices and norms, I seek to advance my knowledge of work in law, culture studies and public interest, and to approach law more generally as a regime for ordering social life, constructing cultural meaning, and shaping group and individual identities.

My diverse work experience and master's degree provide a perfect foundation to tackle the issues faced by a general counsel. At this juncture in my life, I seek more challenge and personal growth in a field that calls on my written skills and attention to detail. My background will bring a unique perspective to the [target law school's] classroom and will make me marketable upon graduation in the field of public interest. By pursuing a law degree, I intend to enter a profession that aligns with the interests and aptitudes I have discovered and developed through my real work experience. It is through deep personal reflection that I have decided that law is the natural extension of my training, personality and talents.

JDMISSION REVIEW

Overall Lesson

Even if you have an extraordinary track record, your personal statement will not write itself.

First Impression

The beginning of the personal statement needs work. On the one hand, the essay is full of potential—the candidate founded a school, which is *really* impressive! Naturally, he would want to discuss what led him to that enormous achievement. On the other hand, mentioning the newspaper articles he wrote is not the best way to introduce his accomplishment. The connection between the candidate's journalistic work and his motivation for founding a school is tenuous and vague to me. He mentions the "mis-education of young Black males," but what does he mean by that? Adding more specifics would strengthen the initial portion of the essay.

Strengths

Clearly, this candidate has a righteous spirit, an entrepreneurial streak, and the ability and commitment to follow through on ideas. I like that he reconsiders his prior views over the course of the essay, which demonstrates that he is capable of growth and humble enough to both change his mind and be upfront about it. The story itself—the founding of the school and the surprising obstacles that shaped his view—is also compelling.

Weaknesses

The candidate needs to do significant work to clarify some of his statements and reinforce the essay's theme so that I understand both *why* he is telling this story and precisely *what happened*. For example, he says he was relentless in finding an audience for his message to "end the destruction of Urban Males," but what exactly does he mean by "destruction"? I can guess what he might be alluding to—issues such as the number of men of color in prisons, the attrition rates in public schools, standardized test scores—but maybe he means something else. I should not have to guess. For this essay to be as powerful as it could be, I need to know what he cares about.

Likewise, the essay is lacking at least one sentence at the end that summarizes how the candidate now views the school he founded. As is, the essay seems unresolved. What is the school's status now? What will happen to it when he leaves to attend law school? In addition, he claims that he began to speak and see things differently, but *how* did doing so lead to his desire to study law? In the essay, he moves from identifying a problem within the community to making an abstract observation about what being the founder of a start-up means. What aspect of his experience will influence his legal (or law-related) career? And how does he plan to use the things he will learn in law school? How will he apply his degree? These elements of his story need to be clarified.

Final Assessment

This personal statement could be quite powerful with an adequate amount of revision. This would have to include heavy attention to grammar and syntax, because the number of errors in this current version is too high for it to be a final draft. As is, the essay is far from ready for submission.

PERSONAL STATEMENT 41

Spell out your ideas concretely.

Once upon a time, a distinguished looking surgeon on television took a snort of white powder—let's presume it was cocaine—just prior to beginning the first incision of a surgery. He had to lift his cloth face mask to get the stuff, no less. This anti-drug commercial from the 1980s was followed in short order by another add featuring an egg cracked open onto a frying pan with the infamous tagline, "This is your brain on drugs."

The oft-mocked "War on Drugs" did impact me (although I'd hate to admit it in certain circles). I was eleven years old and proudly wore my "Just Say No" t-shirt to school and—dare I admit it—even school dances. While in my junior year, I did succumb to the occasional dalliance with alcohol, I am proud and relieved to be able to write that it never blossomed into a habit, and I never tried harder drugs. It did, however, help me to better understand the challenges faced by our youth as they grow up in a world where messages about drugs and alcohol so widely vary.

I remain certain that the education of our youth concerning the risks involved in drug use is the most effective way to decrease the demand for drugs in the future. Nancy Reagan and I remain in full agreement on that point. In fact, if I had my way, those antiquated commercials would make a comeback for a newer and tech savvier generation as a warning about their inherent dangers.

Today, as a drug counselor and social worker, I find I am able to quickly identify individuals with drug dependency problems with very little interaction. The fact that I see people daily who are on one form of drug or another allows me insight into the physical manifestations abusers exhibit. I am more than willing to point it out to them and offer them help. Admittedly, they do not usually accept my offer. But I believe that the more people in my position, with my experience, are willing to make contact with addicts before they have committed a crime or overdosed, the better the chances that a seed might germinate and grow whereby they will eventually seek out help on their own.

Asking my colleagues, doctors and other medical professionals, and reformed addicts to make a pact to make contact with every addict they pass, especially ones that are out of control due to drugs, or even dangerous, might seem unwise. The reasons one would opt out of such a proposition are manifold: 1) Fear of the unknown. 2) Fear of the quiet dangers of approaching an addict. 3) Discomfort due to the fact that nobody likes or respects a buttinsky. 4) The lack of an immediate response after making the effort.

However, I decided to take it upon myself to move forward with this plan. Slowly I began to suggest it to my colleagues and co-workers. I insisted that the more of us who made contact with these addicts in our midst, the more addicts we might keep out of the system altogether.

For sometime I made my case in talks before classrooms of social workers and drug counselors, in AA and NA meetings, and at conferences for medical professionals. There was no way to quantify my success, but my passion continued to grow. Eventually I realized that I wanted a more measurable strategy. I began to investigate legal action groups to help those already trapped inside a failing system. Eventually I got involved with programs like The Addicts Law Project in Chicago and other organizations working to help people victimized by addiction.

I believe that individuals struggling with substance abuse are the ones that didn't get the right messages at the times in their lives when those messages might have set them on a different path. Each of us could easily have become them. And they might have become us. They still could.

I still believe that reaching out to addicts before they hit the system is the best way to help them change their lives. The grassroots-contact movement I started continues to grow to this day. I can't proclaim to have invented a visual as powerful as an egg in a frying pan symbolizing a brain, a coked up surgeon, or even a middle-school meet and greet with t-shirts, but it exists as my own active movement toward change. Now it is time for me to take it to the next level.

jdMission Review

Overall Lesson

Spell out concretely how the story you are telling in your essay has led you to law.

First Impression

This beginning of this essay is neither amazing nor notably problematic. I am not sure why he is invoking the anti-drug campaigns of the 1980s, but I am interested in reading the candidate's story.

Strengths

The candidate has undertaken quite an interesting and powerful project—one that is ambitious, unusual, and socially minded (three attributes that are often the hallmark of top candidates). He has a rich background with which to craft a winning personal statement, and in several paragraphs, he is well on his way. These two paragraphs in particular capture his determination, resilience, and willingness to change course based on outcomes:

> However, I decided to take it upon myself to move forward with this plan. Slowly I began to suggest it to my colleagues and co-workers. I insisted that the more of us who made contact with these addicts in our midst, the more addicts we might keep out of the system altogether.

> For sometime I made my case in talks before classrooms of social workers and drug counselors, in AA and NA meetings, and at conferences for medical professionals. There was no way to quantify my success, but my passion continued to grow. Eventually I realized that I wanted a more measurable strategy. I began to investigate legal action groups to help those already trapped inside a failing sys-

tem. Eventually I got involved with programs like The Addicts Law Project in Chicago and other organizations working to help people victimized by addiction.

Ultimately, however, he does not quite get there; his essay still needs a fair amount of work.

Weaknesses

How did the candidate's "occasional dalliance" with alcohol help him "understand the challenges faced by our youth as they grow up in a world where messages about drugs and alcohol so widely vary"? All I know is that he watched anti-drug ads as a kid, was affected by them, and then himself engaged in underage drinking. What compelled him to drink, and how did doing so lead him to discover the importance of educating youth about the dangers of drugs and alcohol (as he claims it did)?

Likewise, I do not understand the basis for his assertion about the effectiveness of anti-drug ads. He states clearly that they affected *him*, but what evidence does he have to prove that they also influenced *others*?

The paragraph about his interactions with others in his role as a drug counselor and social worker is interesting but not very effective. At first, the candidate seems to be talking about individuals he meets as part of his job, but he is not (and should therefore revise the section to avoid creating this confusion). He is referring to people he encounters outside of the clinic. I find this fascinating— does he actually *approach* people on the street whom he believes are addicts? If so, he should share one of *those* stories. Forget Nancy Reagan!

Finally, what does The Addicts Law Project do? How can the law help addicts, and what did he learn from his work with the legal organizations he mentions? This essay exhibits an all-too-common mistake that applicants make in early drafts of personal statements—referring to a captivating idea but failing to articulate *what that idea actually is*. I want to know more about this project to better understand why this candidate wants to attend law school in the first place.

Final Assessment

I would cut the reference to his drinking in high school; it does not matter, nor does it add any value to the essay. He could retain the reference to the 1980s drug ads, but only if he can better relate them to his overall point—in particular, by providing actual evidence of their effectiveness. And I would advise him to add more specific details about what legal recourse addicts currently have and how he hopes to use the law to further his mission.

PERSONAL STATEMENT 42

Create a balance between narrative and reflection.

It isn't that I never got wasted, I mean, I was the bass player in the band. But I just never did it like Kevin Merrymen. Merrymen was the front man for Harper's Ferry Demolition, or HFD if you were local and knew the scene. I met him at a friend's party when he was in college and I was newly graduated from music school. Boston is a place where you are always either in school, or just leaving it. For me, I'd grown up there, and then stayed to study guitar and eventually focus on bass.

Of course HFD wasn't my first band. I had been playing since I was eleven with some talented people over the years. But when I met Merrymen, there was just something different about that guy. We'd just turned over into the new millennium and I had a feeling the world was about to get pretty big. I took meeting him as a sign. He'd been drinking that night, but we all had. Soon Peters got out his guitar and soon everyone was beating on anything that made an interesting sound. Suddenly Merrymen, un-mic'd, started howling these lyrics overtop of the Jam connecting with almost every corner of sound in that room and tying it together. I had never heard anything like it, before or since.

I suspect I wasn't the only one either. Years later people still talked about that jam and how it had impacted their lives. If you've never had that kind of moment with music, you should really go about spending the rest of your life trying to replicate it. But one thing was definite: No one left the room that day without hoping that Kevin Merrymen would front a band.

Six months later Mike Nagel left the Fallovers and we started up Harper's Ferry Demolition. Before we'd even penned our first song we were already booked at two bars in Jamaica Plain and one in Brookline. We brought in drums and had a five-person band. The music poured out of us. One year in we were guaranteeing bars a sellout. But that was also when we started to lose the thread.

First the label came to a show. We had warning, which might have been just the impetus for imploding that Merrymen needed. But I'll never forget how my heart broke and my stomach twisted up in knots when he showed up on stage three hours late, puke in his hair, screaming out words over our music that shattered it into shards of unlistenable glass, bleeding out our eardrums. I woke up the next morning devastated.

When I confronted him, I had Nagel and Peters with me. Merrymen was snorting blow with our drummer and two half-naked girls who looked alarmingly young. He didn't look like he had slept or bathed in days. He was covered in stink.

"Son," I began, looking him dead on, "My folks are immigrants, my skin is brown, I ain't got shots in life like you've got."

His unfocused eyes wobbled around trying to land on my face.

I continued, "You are my one shot, man. You gotta aim me, son. You gotta start up again."

Merrymen didn't respond. Two days later he showed up for rehearsal dry as a California riverbed. Two weeks later, he fell off the wagon.

Harper's Ferry Demolition put out one album that made six "Best of 2000" lists, including one in a weekly publication in Paris, France. Even today, some people in the Boston music scene know exactly what it means when someone says, "Careful you don't pull a Merrymen." You better not fall apart, squander your talent, or ruin it for your band.

Because of the short-but-sweet success of HFD, I was able to play for many years in bands around the world. I loved that I have been able to spend so long living that dream. But I never loved music again the way I did when I was playing it with HFD. Over time, playing became more of a job and less of a passion. I realized then that the speech I had given my old friend Merrymen—wherever he is—that night after he threw away the label, had proved decidedly incorrect. Merrymen was never my one shot. *I* always was. I'm the one that has always had to aim myself.

Starting up again is exactly what I plan to do with an education in law. I was already the first person to whom I am related by blood to graduate college and enjoy a steady career. Now, I am ready to go one even better. Merrymen might have had the music, but I've got the gift.

jdMission Review

Overall Lesson

Strike a balance between narration and reflection.

First Impression

Although I like the easy tone and the sincere start, I think referencing one's "getting wasted" in a first sentence is a bad idea. I also just do not think that doing so is needed after reading the second sentence. He could start with "Keven Merrymen was…" and achieve the same result. Overall, this essay reads like a decent first draft that could use some serious revision.

Strengths

The narrative here is strong; I want to keep reading to find out what happens to the band. Likewise, the thesis that the applicant's opportunities for success do not depend on a single person or instance is a powerful idea, strong and universal enough to ground an essay. That said, he spends so much time telling the story of the band's rise and fall that he misses an opportunity to elaborate on that theme in an effective way early enough in the essay.

Weaknesses

The story about the band is too long. It can be condensed to about two-thirds if not one-half the length and have the same effect. In particular, the parts where the narrator quotes himself are slightly jarring—the way he speaks to his bandmate is strikingly different from how he writes. This could be resolved by just describing his conversation with Merrymen rather than quoting himself.

By shortening the story, the applicant could devote more space to his self-discovery that he is powerful in his own right and more space linking that discovery to his interest in a legal career.

Also, the following paragraph is confusing, because I do not know who showed up with puke in his hair—the label or Merrymen?

> First the label came to a show. We had warning, which might have been just the impetus for imploding that Merrymen needed. But I'll never forget how my heart broke and my stomach twisted up in knots when he showed up on stage three hours late, puke in his hair, screaming out words over our music that shattered it into shards of unlistenable glass, bleeding out our eardrums...

I eventually figure out that the writer is talking about Merrymen, but the way he has written it is unclear.

Finally, this essay has various misuses of vocabulary that are problematic in ways that Microsoft Word will not recognize. For example, "overtop" is a verb but not a preposition, which is how it has been used here. This illustrates the importance of having others proofread your work—the word "overtop" was not underlined in squiggly red by Microsoft, but that does not mean it was used correctly. Other problems here include that "replicate" is used incorrectly and "started up" should just be "started" or "founded."

We cannot stress this enough: have someone else—with good grammar skills—read your essay!

Final Assessment

The skeleton of a strong personal statement can be found here—a clear, compelling personal narrative, and an extraction of meaning from it that is relevant to a legal career. But as is, the narrative component is given way too much space, while the meaning component is given too little. A better balance must be found between narration and reflection. As is, I finish the essay wondering, "Does he really want to go to law school? Why does he not keep pursuing music?"

Personal Statement 43

Watch for excessive sentimentality.

Growing up with a younger brother who suffered from a chronic seizure and heart condition helped me develop an acute sense of responsibility towards those in need. Oftentimes, my desire to help others required personal sacrifices. After I graduated college in 2010, I decided to indefinitely postpone my plans to attend graduate school in order to help my family's struggling flower business. After two years of working as a florist, I started to question whether I would ever be back in a classroom again. In the summer of 2012, I embarked on a two-week long medical mission trip to Peru, with the belief that serving others would help me refocus my life.

By 4 PM on the last day of our trip, we had distributed all of the medicine, but there were still many villagers who were waiting on line. As the remaining villagers dejectedly walked away from our campsite, I could not help but feel like I had personally failed. My heart ached. For these villagers, our medication and treatment was the only form of primary care that they would ever receive. My conscience was burdened by the thought of leaving them behind, still in pain. As we began loading the bus to leave, a little girl named Sidra and her family entered through the rusted schoolyard gate.

She sprinted towards me, while her mother and grandmother apologetically followed in tow. *¡Dulces! ¡Dulces!* She demanded candy, and lots of it. I greeted her family and explained to them that they had unfortunately come too late, and that we no longer had any candy or medicine left over. As Sidra began to cry, her mother and grandmother apologized on behalf of the child and began to walk away with their shoulders sunken in at their sides. The finality in the way that they walked away from our camp stirred me to action.

I ran over to Sidra's mother and firmly cupped both of her hands in mine. She and I were both startled by the directness of my action. Now, almost in tears, I pleaded with her: "I don't have medicine and I don't have candy, but is there any other way that I can help you?" She tightened her grip and smiled. I startled her again as I began to pour out the contents of my backpack in front of her. I picked up the two granola bars and bag of almonds that had fallen out and gave them to Sidra. A smile on her face blossomed. But it wasn't enough. I wanted to do something more for this family. I was looking for Tylenol when I found an unopened package of Korean pain relief patches in the front pocket of my backpack. I asked Sidra's grandmother where she was hurting and I placed the patches on her wrist and back. Shortly thereafter, my team called for me from the bus and in what felt like a blur of a moment, I held Sidra, her mother, and her grandmother in a teary embrace, thanking them.

I always thought that I needed a better channel to translate my desire to help others, and my experience in Peru solidified this. Whenever my heart would be burdened by the same inconsolable feeling of not being able to help those most in need of protection, I acted. After years of seeing my mother crying at the hospital because she was unable to communicate in English with my brother's doctors and nurses, I studied Korean rigorously and began translating for my family. When my brother was diagnosed with a heart condition in my senior year of high school, I chose an undergraduate institution that was close to home in order to be available in case of emergencies. When I found out that many of my fellow church members were being forced to leave the country because of visa issues, I used my bilingual abilities to tutor them in English, and prep them for interviews with potential employers. After I began working as a corporate recruiter, I actively sought out companies that were willing to sponsor these individuals with H1-B visas.

Eventually, my desire to serve others became second nature to me. So much so that I was unable to recognize that it had also developed into a passion and a reason for why I wanted to go to law school. Sidra and her family eventually helped me realize this. I saw my own family and community in Sidra's family. As they began to walk away, I asked myself whether I would be able to leave my own family behind in good conscience if they were in the same position as Sidra's. I already knew the answer, and yet that was exactly what I was about to do. Although my team and I were able to provide some relief to the villagers, I knew that it was only a temporary solution. I couldn't help but feel like there was only so much that I could do as one individual.

Until now, I have been relying on my own efforts to help others. However, I believe that the law can empower me in a way that transcends my limitations as an individual, and help me expand my reach. I hope to one day be able to promote systematic changes through improving the legal and policy frameworks that protect whole communities. I believe that this is the next logical step in my life's commitment to serving others. I hope that through a formal legal education and training, I will be better equipped to protect and serve those who are most in need of protection, both domestically and abroad.

JdMission Review

Overall Lesson

Avoid sentimentality.

First Impression

The candidate's first paragraph is concise and informative. It moves at a quick pace but does not omit important details, which can be a difficult balance to achieve. I am therefore immediately impressed with his writing skills (though he should say "often" rather than "oftentimes"). I also am looking forward to learning more about his life in the rest of the essay.

Strengths

The candidate has some great material to work with, and a few of his paragraphs are excellent. His strong writing skills shine throughout the essay.

Weaknesses

The sentence "For these villagers, our medication and treatment was the only form of primary care that they would ever receive" involves too extreme of a claim. Take care to avoid making statements like this. The candidate cannot actually know that the assistance his team has provided will be the only primary care the villagers *ever* receive. What if other groups like his provide aid in the future? What if, in the best-case scenario, a medical facility is built in the village? Making predictions about the lives of others, especially in such absolute terms, can sound patronizing.

Another language issue appears in this sentence: "As Sidra began to cry, her mother and grandmother apologized on behalf of the child and began to walk away with their shoulders sunken in at their sides." Be wary of invoking clichés in this way—using the phrase "sunken shoulders" to describe someone who is sad is so common that it can sound cartoonish, and you certainly do not want to seem as though you are objectifying the people in your story. The candidate should instead try to remember and more authentically describe how the family members *actually* looked, apart from their slumped shoulders, and if he cannot, he should simply say something along the lines of "I could sense their disappointment as they walked away."

Likewise, some of the language choices in the fourth paragraph give the essay a level of sentimentality that does not work very well. The candidate sounds a bit self-centered when he describes himself as being "almost in tears"—*he* is not the impoverished one in the story—so I would remove that phrase. Also, simply saying that the girl smiled is better than saying that her smile "blossomed" (another cliché). Finally, he should cut the description of the embrace at the end of the paragraph. Although I have no doubt that this was a meaningful moment for the candidate, the description of it borders on self-absorbed. Fortunately, the paragraph is just as effective—actually, more so—without this sentence.

Final Assessment

Once the candidate removes some of the sentimentality from the middle of the essay, his personal statement will be quite good. He delivers his theme in the last sentence of the penultimate paragraph: "Although my team and I were able to provide some relief to the villagers, I knew that it was only a temporary solution. I couldn't help but feel like there was only so much that I could do as one individual." If the candidate can arrive at this idea in a well-supported way, and without too much melodrama, he will have a strong essay to submit for consideration.

PERSONAL STATEMENT 44

Quadruple-check your grammar.

Our world changed forever, not just for Americans but for everyone, I am referring to when the United States (US) economy crashed in September 2008. In that time, I was beginning my religious studies at Columbia International University (CIU) in Columbia, SC. While I was a full-time seminarian, I was also working full-time as a Registered Nurse at Carolinas Medical Center in Charlotte, NC in a position that paid a per diem rate. At this point in my life I thought I was doing pretty well for myself, as I was 26 years old, a single woman, who was ambitious, driven, and had her 5-, 10-, and 15 year plan on cruise control. In addition, I was a homeowner in Charlotte, NC. As I was a residing in Charlotte, I was commuting back and forth to Columbia, SC for class which was almost a two hour drive each way.

Yet, this story had a major shift when in 2009; I had to leave my job due to lack of available hours. Then in 2011, I was unable to finish my seminary studies due to finances. On top of all that the stress of my economic situation began to take a toll on my health. Then in 2012, my home of 5 years was foreclosed on. At this point, I was 30 years old woman who had a promising future, but yet had lost everything I had worked hard for and saw as my trophies for all my achievements.

But in the end, all I had left was my faith, my education, and my determination to not allow my life to be paralyzed by these extreme economic hardships. If it was not for the prayers and support of my family, I do not know how I would have made it through this tough time. For months, I kept replaying these experiences over in my mind in trying to figure out what mistakes did I make to get to this point, and if I did not make any mistakes then why did this have to happen to me. I did everything I could to prevent these horrible events from taking place. I used all my resources and educated myself to the best of my ability to prevent such events from taking place in my life.

But all with no avail, I had to come to the realization that I did lose it all and that there was nothing else I could do to have prevent it from happening or to have changed the course of events. When I did finally accept the fact, which took me a long time to do, I said I would use all that I went through to make me a stronger and wiser person. In addition, I believe I did not go through all these hardships for myself, but to be able to relate to others who have had such experiences or are experiencing very trying times in their own lives.

Since 2010, I had a growing, burning desire to go to law school but one thing after another made me doubt myself and my ability to achieve such a goal as law school because of its extreme rigorousness and demanding academic commitment, more so than nursing school. Yet, even during my hardships, my desire to seek a career in the legal profession grew even more with further clarity about why I had to go through what I went through. I have always seen the importance of advocacy, but now I see it in a broader sense in that advocacy is not just about speaking up for others but having the passion and drive to fight for the rights of others at any cost.

Therefore, if my experiences have helped me to overcome the fear and doubt of accepting my fate in pursuing a career in the legal profession then in a bitter-sweet way it was worth it. These experiences will in turn make me a much more effective, efficient, compassionate, and dedicated professional in the legal field. In addition, I will be able to impact my community on a local, national, and global level.

I am determined now more than ever to move forward in seeking a legal education at Harvard Law School (HLS) for the school's history and reputation as well as its commitment to public service by providing legal aid to the local community, such as your past initiatives in assisting local residents with foreclosures. I have always been community oriented and I commend the school for making it a requirement for each student to have a certain number of pro bono service hours to graduate from HLS. I cannot think of any other school that would prepare me for my future in the legal profession then at HLS. Therefore, I do hope that the Admissions Committee will see my passion and commitment in having to overcome many challenges and hardships to reach this decision in my life in wanting to become a lawyer.

JdMission Review

Overall Lesson

In the climax of your essay (the big transition), avoid vagueness and use concrete language instead.

First Impression

The beginning of this essay is too dramatic. A better choice would be to say, "When the U.S. economy crashed in September 2008, I was beginning my religious studies at Columbia International University in Columbia, SC." As the essay continues, it feels very plot heavy—the candidate tells us what happened to her, but she does not really convey her thoughts about what was happening apart from "I thought I was doing pretty well for myself." In addition to being too informal, this statement does not describe what was going on in her mind. Why was she working full-time as a nurse while also attending school full-time out of town? Why did she have a two-hour commute? Why was she not living in the city where she attended school or going to school in the city where she lived? We need to know the reasons behind her choices and to understand how her experiences affected her emotionally. She could share her insights by describing her hopes at that time and what she envisioned accomplishing in five years.

Strengths

The candidate comes across as 100% truthful. Her story is painful to read, and many Americans could probably relate to it. She also effectively illustrates her reasoning for wanting to attend law school: she lost her job and her house. She seems to have been without an advocate during her foreclosure, so now she wants to become a legal advocate for others. That is a powerful experience.

Weaknesses

Before she describes the rough patch in her life, she needs to reflect more on the events leading up to it and share her emotional reality. Once the candidate presents her decision to attend law school, we need more concrete details. Did she in fact have a lawyer during her foreclosure? Why did she decide not to resume her religious studies? She says that in 2009, her financial stress began to "take a toll" on her health, but she does not explain what that toll was. I am sure she has answers, but we need more concrete details about her story for this essay to feel complete.

Also, her grammar is problematic enough to be an obstacle for her as both a law student and a lawyer, but even before then as a law school applicant. Her essay contains numerous run-on sentences. In the short term, she should have someone with excellent grammatical skills line edit her work. In the long term, she should take a grammar class or invest in a grammar book. Although the work will likely be tedious and dull initially, she will ultimately learn the fundamentals, and doing so will serve her well for the rest of her life and career.

Final Assessment

I would advise this candidate to consider the questions I have posed in this review and then work the answers into her essay. She should then ask a trusted person to review it line by line and identify and discuss any grammatical problems he/she finds. She has a wonderful and powerful essay buried somewhere in here—she just needs to dig it out and polish it!

PERSONAL STATEMENT 45

Strike duplicate information.

It is the first of July, 2014 and CIA along with DIA intelligence shows that Kim Jung-Un has purged three of his top generals and that the North Korean army is on the march towards the demilitarized zone. North Korea has been diverting foreign aid funds and assets from sanctioned uses to their military, subsequently forcing countries to reduce or end their foreign aid programs to North Korea. Relations with South Korea have stalled and forced an eight percent drop in trade between the two countries. As a member of a DIA intelligence analysis group focused on the increasingly hostile situation in North Korea, I was tasked to assess the intentions of the Kim regime and advise future action of the United States.

During my junior year of undergraduate study, I had the immense pleasure of working on a project that involved acting as an intelligence analyst for the DIA in a team of four, while another group of four acted as intelligence analyst for the CIA as we analyzed fictitious intelligence reports on North Korea and the Kim regime. We were tasked to pore through the intelligence given to us, be it satellite images of military movements, economic reports on the country, or notices of executions of some of the top generals in the country. With the training we had received all semester we ultimately assessed the situation and gave our thoughts along with a presentation to the "President," who in reality was the chairman of the political science department at my university.

The project entailed that the four of us would have to work together to assess the situation and brief the "President." The team leader would acquire the intelligence and assign each of us a certain aspect of it to work on. We would then come together and discuss the intelligence we had. We agreed on a set of assumptions to frame our analysis on and then began to assess the situation. I created an assessment from the group and briefed the "President" on the situation; all the while the other team did the same. Ultimately, my team concluded with moderate confidence that the degrading economic situation in the Democratic People's Republic of Korea [DPRK] influenced the new Kim regime to pursue military action against South Korea in order to remain sovereign and to possibly reunite the Korean peninsula, or to capture Seoul so as to negotiate for beneficial concessions for the DPRK.

This undergraduate exercise stirred my interest in international and national security law. With the intelligence community describing situations that could arise, national leaders must make decisions based on the assessments given to them, but also must worry about the legality of their actions and if they have the power to do anything while maintaining relationships with affected countries. [Law School Name]'s program [name of program] brings this to light and teaches those involved how to handle the situation, granting hands on experience in the national security and international law fields. Involvement in this program would offer me not only experience in the field, but also a rewarding chance to further my interest of national security and international relations.

With my background in International Relations and having taken classes on topics such as war and politics, intelligence assessment, and the nature of terrorism and how to combat it, pursing a law degree and working as legal counsel to administrations and agencies devoted to issues that arise between nations and national security would enable me to have a tangible impact in such situations. A degree from [Law School Name] with a focus in national security or international law would enable me to pursue a career in this field. My previous classroom experiences in related fields give me a concrete foundation to build upon in law school and have given me skills to be successful in law school as well as the real world.

jdMission Review

Overall Lesson

Use your limited space wisely—cut duplicate information to make room for other vital details.

First Impression

The candidate's topic is fascinating, and his essay has a very catchy beginning. Note that the story he has elected to share works only because it involves an actual classroom experience he had in college. If he were instead describing and predicting what he believes *could* happen in North Korea and therefore simply sharing his personal thoughts on the issue, that would be odd and probably not a good idea.

Strengths

This personal statement features unique content with clear ties to the candidate's interest in law school.

Weaknesses

To start, what is the DIA? I do not know—which means admissions officers might not know either. To avoid any confusion or missed information caused by unclear abbreviations like this, the candidate should write out the full name of the organization—the Defense Intelligence Agency—at first use and then introduce the abbreviation or acronym (if it will be used again later in the essay) so the reader does not have to turn to Google. Also, the candidate switches from present tense to past tense in the last line of the first paragraph; he should maintain the same tense throughout his story.

In addition, the candidate needs to provide more background information on this undergraduate exercise. First, he needs to reveal sooner that his story is about a political science class. Second, given that the assignment was fictional, what were his information sources? More details would allow me to better understand this project. And because the essay contains some duplicate information that the candidate can easily cut (e.g., we are told twice that his group researched and analyzed the situation and then briefed the "President"), doing so will create space he can then use to elaborate on the project and reflect on its meaning to him.

Finally, I would strike "real world" from the last sentence. This phrase is used far too often in law school personal statements.

Final Assessment

The last paragraph works overall. Unlike many people who profess an interest in international law and international relations without the background to support a career in those fields, this candidate demonstrates relevant experience. By sharing the story of—and his enthusiasm for—this academic assignment, he demonstrates that he was engaged in the exercise.

PERSONAL STATEMENT 46

Cut out extraneous details.

There are times in life when we happen upon a crossroads, a path split in two and we must choose a direction in which to go. These crossroads become meaningful when choosing one path over another changes your life. But there are other life changing paths that we do not choose. They are chosen for us. We are beckoned toward or pushed into them, and every day thereafter, we are inevitably bound to that dusty trail.

When I was fifteen, my cousin borrowed her half-sister's yellow Ford to drive us to King's Castle, an amusement park that boasted seven roller coasters, including her favorite, The Spiral Vortex, which featured six inversion loops, including a double corkscrew. It was my first time at the park, but my cousin's family, my mom's sister and her husband, his two kids, a boy and a girl, and her two kids, my actual cousins, both girls, were regulars.

We arrived just before open and after buying our tickets, immediately tore through the park until we got to the modest line of the enormous coaster, only seven people deep. We would get to ride on the first train of the day. My cousin was thrilled. I tried to absorb some of her excitement, but my fear was overwhelming. By the time they began to load us into the car, I was near tears.

"I think I'll wait," I told her. "I want to warm up on something first."

But she grabbed my arm, and I followed her into the third seat of the in-sect-like contraption and clicked the harness into place over my head. I gripped the red padded leather tightly to me and closed my eyes. We hadn't even moved yet.

Slowly the train pulled out and after a sharp turn, began its ascent. We could see the entire park from our seats. The train clicked leisurely up the hill, betraying the onslaught it was about to put forth. The silence when we reached the pinnacle was near-deafening. As the coaster roared to its maximum speed I lost function in every part of my body. I tried to inhale, but the pressure was profound.

We looped through the first inversion and then the second in quick succession. I hadn't counted. I was told this information later. It was the third of the Vortex corkscrews that got it. I could only have said it was somewhere between the first and fiftieth that locked us in.

We rolled up the next loop on the track and then it simply stopped in place. There was no sputter or gurgle. No grunt or clack. The train rolled upward and then stopped exactly where it decided to stop. My reaction wasn't immediate. Like I said, my emotions were as trapped deep down under my skin as I was now trapped upside-down on this roller coaster. My neck was elongated, gravity pressing my head toward the ground that was fifty-feet below, another fact I read days later in a newspaper article that recounted that day. I would have guessed a much higher number. I could feel my blood gathering in the crown of my head. Time all kind of came together but at some point, someone shouted, "I'm slipping!" But her voice was muddled by the voices of other passengers calling out for release, including my own. At minute seven, which I also learned later, another voice joined hers in raising the alarm. "Help!" those two voices yelled. "She's slipping!"

The voices were several rows behind me. My own mobility was limited. But sometime later I learned that the two people in front and the two people behind the twenty-two-year-old had tried to form some kind of net of arms to hold her up as her red harness failed and clicked out of position. I don't remember her face from the line or from when we boarded. I only remember it the way everyone else does, peering out with a broad pretty smile from the newspaper article that immortalized her.

When she fell at minute 7, second 43, according to the paper, I closed my eyes and heard her screaming. I could hear the sobs of her friend. The rest of the eighteen minutes slugged by until at last the car seamlessly slid down the corkscrew and flew unhindered across seven more. Finally we landed back at the beginning and the Spiral Vortex closed down for two months as her parents tried to make sense of the death of their child.

We were each ushered into the care of a team of EMS personnel and checked for injuries. We were asked to sign something that a lawyer who'd been riding at the front, suggested none of us sign without having a lawyer look it over. We later learned that our tickets waived much of King's Castle's responsibility. But in the end there was a settlement that each of the thirteen rider's split after a trial that awarded the victim's parent's a little more money, but no new child.

I finished high school and college, certain that I would one day apply to law school. I would make sure that those who needed accountability would be held accountable. There are times when we are forced down paths we never wanted, or never needed to go down. Sometimes those paths are unavoidable. But one more test ride around the Spiral Vortex might have saved a life that day. Attention to the safety harness and an assurance of its viability might have kept that girl alive.

I believe in the laws of our nation in keeping each of us safe and secure. I believe in the future of our nation and the promise it holds, in spite of the eighteen minutes I spent upside down, fifty-feet up, held in place a by a harness that only just happened to work.

JDMISSION REVIEW

Overall Lesson

The details of horrific events can often be spared to make room for adequate, relevant reflection.

First Impression

The first paragraph of the essay sounds a little cliché to me and does not really say anything. She can strike it altogether.

Strengths

Wow—what a horrifying story. The candidate's writing is strong. She delivers an effective narrative (effective in the sense that I needed to stand up and walk around to shake off my emotions after reading it). Her "take-away"—for lack of a more sensitive word—from her tragic experience at the amusement park is plausible and touching: she wants to be a lawyer. I am not surprised.

Weaknesses

The beginning of the essay does not really prepare the reader for what happens in the end. I initially think I am about to read about a young girl's first roller coaster ride, and I am not ready for what the true story turns out to be instead. She does not need to tell us up front that someone dies, but she could bring readers into the action sooner and cut some of the extraneous details, such as "my cousin's family, my mom's sister and her husband, his two kids, a boy and a girl, and her two kids, my actual cousins, both girls"—we do not need to know all of that. We also do not need to be told that her cousin borrowed her half-sister's car. And we do not need to hear quite so much about what happened leading up to their ride on the roller coaster.

In addition, language like this is too forced: "The train clicked leisurely up the hill, betraying the onslaught it was about to put forth." The candidate needs to tell her story in a voice that sounds more genuine. The truth is, when chronicling a tragic event like this one, you should use language sparsely. The event speaks for itself; you do not need to add drama by writing flowery sentences. Just describe what happened.

Finally, this compelling and heartbreaking story no doubt had an enormous impact on the candidate's life, and she could strengthen the essay by devoting more space to discussing *what* that impact was rather than simply describing the details of the accident. Despite her gripping account of the tragic incident, the essay would be more effective if the candidate described how it fueled her interest in law. Was she angry about the outcome of the case or about the amusement park's attempt to avoid liability? She implies that something in this vein was upsetting to her, but she does not tell us what exactly that was. By that point in the essay, I am eager to read her reflections on that aspect of the event.

Final Assessment

To be more balanced, this essay needs some revision at the beginning to eliminate the crossroads-related clichés and some elaboration at the end to more clearly explain the accident's role in the candidate's decision to attend law school. With this work, the essay could become as powerful as the story it tells.

PERSONAL STATEMENT 47

Have someone else
read your essay.

I don't think I understood about being black. Everyone in my world just was. Of course there were white people and black people, but race and its complexities seemed to play out mostly on TV, in movies, in newspapers. But in my world, and let me try not to sound cliché, there were just deepening and lightening shades of people.

Mr. Siegel owned the bodega in Brooklyn where I had my first job stocking condiments and toilet paper. I understood why we kept that toilet paper but things like pickles and canned beets always confounded me. Here we had 400 square feet to keep on hand important last-minute items. Somehow I could never imagine someone running into a late night canned beet emergency.

Mr. Siegel's skin was sort of milky gray. I certainly wouldn't call him "white." He was mostly kind except when he was hungover and then he just grunted. But he was never mean or disrespectful.

Mary Johnson was our neighbor. I called her ma'am. Her skin was lilac purple with ashy elbows. Lisa worked by the Utica train station and always stopped the high school kids and introduced herself so you'd know you had someone looking out for you. Her skin was sandy brown and her eyes were green. She spoke Spanish to the Latina kids and my best friend from high school Diego who is Dominican said she told him a really funny joke that just didn't translate to English. I tried to get her to tell me but instead she said I'd have to wait until I learned Spanish.

Billy had skin like coffee with a tiny bit of milk. My first girlfriend Melissa had pink skin that smelled like oatmeal with honey and cream. My mama's skin was gray and gold depending on how the sun shone on her. And my sister, Tara, had skin the color of roasted almonds.

I left Brooklyn and came to Pennsylvania, where I felt my blackness like a hole in the middle of an expansive white sea. I looked around and felt invisible, like I'd somehow suck all the light out of any room I'd enter. I thought they couldn't see me, the color of my skin, a dulled and muted shade of theirs. I suddenly understood about being black, and I didn't like what I was understanding.

The silence of my first month of college was profound and colorless. Until slowly, in classes I'd raise my hand and speak and eyes would find me, or maybe they already had. In fact, I began to see that they had seen me all along. It was me that for the first time had discovered a color in me. It was the color of my own fear and prejudice. One by one I met the individuals. And everything I saw went from a vast sea of white to a giant sea shaded by many colors, faces and people.

I want to be a lawyer so that I can suss out the details, go beyond the stereotypes we see when we meet someone for the first time or walk into a new room, or leave the neighborhood where we grow up. It fills me with fire to think that the job of a lawyer is to break each fact down to its smallest part and reveal something that once seemed cut and dry—black and white—is in fact different shades across a spectrum.

Broad strokes might be easier to see, a grabbed image to which you attach all your preconceived ideas. Details are harder to spot and remember. They require consideration, patience and a willingness to look closely. For the world and even more, for myself, I will continue to notice our details, and I will draw attention to them for others.

JDMISSION REVIEW

Overall Lesson

Have someone else read your personal statement to help you smooth any rough patches.

First Impression

The basic idea behind this essay is great: the candidate did not understand what "being black" meant until he went to college. However, the way he expresses this idea in his opening sentence ("I don't think I understood about being black.") does not work well. The same goes for the last clause of the first paragraph, which reads, "there were just deepening and lightening shades of people." Saying "deeper" and "lighter" shades instead would make more sense.

Strengths

Overall, the essay is strong. I like the theme, which is that for a long time, he did not "see" color, then he *did* see it, and finally, he learned to look past it. And the idea that his ability to observe detail and nuance is fueling his interest in law is a nice tie-in. I particularly like the idea he expresses here: "Broad strokes might be easier to see, a grabbed image to which you attach all your preconceived ideas. Details are harder to spot and remember. They require consideration, patience and a willingness to look closely."

But despite the candidate's affinity for details, his essay could still use a hearty edit!

Weaknesses

The candidate uses some phrasings that simply do not read smoothly and could therefore be distracting or even confusing to a reader. I mentioned two such instances in the First Impression section of this review, and this issue persists throughout the essay, in some places more than others. For example, the candidate writes, "It was me that for the first time had discovered a color in me." A better way of phrasing this would be to say, "I was the one who, for the first time, had begun to see my own color."

This sentence has the same problem: "I suddenly understood about being black, and I didn't like what I was understanding." A more effective wording would be "I suddenly understood what it meant to 'be black,' and I didn't like it."

Final Assessment

This candidate needs to have someone with excellent editing skills and a keen eye review his essay. Every sentence should read clearly, and every subject and verb should match flawlessly. The ideas are there, and the scenes he describes are visually compelling—he just needs to work on polishing and finessing the prose a bit.

Personal Statement 48

Eliminate the cursing,
self-deprecation, and romance.

Lately I've begun figuring out that the time in history during which I have lived has to be the very best one. I think, for example how fabulous it feels to have been born still during the time of the typewriter and in the days when people still dressed to fly, if only just barely. I have begun thinking about the moments between moments—moments without greatness or genius, unsurprising, just-people-moments. With no great love, or even great desire. But there is no absence of them either, just not enough to warrant commentary or narrative. I am alone, but also, hardly alone. I notice myself only insomuch as I relate to my compromised history.

The relationship with my last boyfriend virtually began with a break up. Several weeks in it had the appearance of a mediocre firefly with its light only ever half-on. It had become my very own ongoing monologue, an attempt to dictate my way into love. I pointed out *everything;* what I liked, what I didn't like. I asked him for his approval, disapproval, I asked, How are you feeling? What do you think about this? How do you feel about god, love, sex, cinema, soup and the paranormal?

I may not have snuffed out any possibility of love, but I certainly made it very difficult. I greased up the windows. I took out the sparkle, smothered the mystery. I even began to sound to myself like a goddamned Edward Albee play.

But it was true. Before he had time to think, "She sure does make a great roast chicken," I would be all over him asking aloud, "Do you like it?" "Isn't it good?" "What does it taste like to you?" Until the thing became so up-close and deconstructed, it didn't taste like anything at all...

He dumped me by way of a phone call. He used a line about his ex-girlfriend, explaining that she was thinking of moving to town and that she'd been thinking about him. He presented the situation as if somehow I was the one coming between *them*, as if he and I hadn't been together every day for the last eight months.

He said something along the lines of, "I really think I owe it to her to try."

I was walking...In fact, I remember I walked by a bookstore and it seemed so mundane, a window full of cookbooks! There was one book with a picture of a man holding a cartoon chicken and I remember I laughed at it out loud, so he said, "She and I had a very important thing!" very serious, as if to imply

I was making fun of his great love. After eight months! *Months*. And all along he'd been thinking of her, considering her.

Three weeks later he reversed his message. He began calling and apologizing and telling me he did it "wrong," meaning he should have probably gone home to see her without having told me, left me on deck, like a pitcher, like a lounge chair. It was on another call during which I was asking for my red shirt and some music he had borrowed when we'd first started dating. And my dignity, I asked him to look around for it because I couldn't seem to find it and just maybe I'd left it at his place.

He told me how it had gone with his ex and how she'd filled the room with her moans of dissatisfaction and cigarette smoke. He said he missed what was so clean and contained about me. I made sure to tell him about the two dates I had set up for next week.

And then I became the girl in his bed in the desperate invention of an opposite of loneliness. I no longer expected love. I no longer needed to coax it verbally out of its favorite darkened hole. In exchange for the silence came the festering understanding that suddenly there were blizzards of disrespectful fucks painting piss stained snowdrifts on all the fire hydrants of my life, and how that came to be, I would never understand. Where had I gone wrong?

After another three months, I finally ended it. But there was something about this loss that made a final break in my cynical heart. One thing I know for sure, I am bold when I stop believing: Like the cigarettes and alcohol of those lady's with the saddest eyes, like the man who double checks his suicide with an overdose and a noose.

Finally I left it all behind completely, which is the simple way to say that I severed myself into two distinct people, the one who was, and the one who is. Mindfully, I made a decision to become a hand held out to people in the clutches of relationships from which they cannot let go. There are no more lessons within a tragedy you choose than there are truths in someone else's living lie. I began my life positioned to understand the law behind love, relationship comings and goings and *changings*.

Of course there has always been my limitless future. It has become clear that, for example, I don't believe in great art. I think it strives to perfect upon nature, but in the end becomes a bad imitation of its impreciseness. Music, for example mimicking the inevitable beauty of the sound of traffic patterns in the rain. The copycatting of accidental side-effects, well, frankly it just makes me sad for all of us. But when it comes to art and love and beauty, the only container, the only boundary and weight is the law. So I will use it and therefore build the verbal container for which I have been and always will be searching.

JDMISSION REVIEW

Overall Lesson

Curse only sparingly, disparage your present-day self even more sparingly, and in general, avoid dramatic tales of romance.

First Impression

When I am reading this kind of essay, I have to stop at a certain point and ask myself, "Is what I am reading brilliant or incoherent?" Often, the line between the two is a very fine one. Unfortunately, my impression at the end of the first paragraph of this essay is *incoherent*. I am not saying that the candidate's *thinking* is incoherent—her thoughts may be beautiful and full of insight, and some of her phrasing suggests as much. But my initial assessment is that her thoughts sound like gobbledygook, and I find myself hoping for her sake (and mine) that the essay will improve as I continue reading.

Strengths and Weaknesses

This essay's greatest strength is also its greatest weakness. So for this review, I have combined these two categories.

On the one hand, I find myself so enraptured by her writing that I forget I am reading a personal statement. I feel as though I have just stumbled across someone's diary at a flea market and am discovering her secrets.

On the other hand, *because* I feel as though I have just stumbled across someone's diary at a flea market and am discovering her secrets, I pause and ask myself, "Wait…does this person belong in law school?"

Take, for example, these lines: "I may not have snuffed out any possibility of love, but I certainly made it very difficult. I greased up the windows. I took out the sparkle, smothered the mystery. I even began to sound to myself like a goddamned Edward Albee play."

These sentences read like a confessional in the *New York Times'* Modern Love column, *not* like part of a law school application, in which, generally speaking, you should refrain from cursing, berating yourself, and sharing the details of your messy past relationships. (Note that an exception could be made for cases in which romantic drama is unquestionably relevant to the applicant's theme and that theme is relevant to his/her law school candidacy—but this is not one of those cases.)

And finally, this application of her thought process to the law is confusing: "But when it comes to art and love and beauty, the only container, the only boundary and weight is the law. So I will use it and therefore build the verbal container for which I have been and always will be searching."

Huh?

In some places in this essay, the candidate writes abstractly very well. However, this particular instance is not one of them, nor do I think abstraction is necessarily appropriate when she finally shifts her discussion to the topic of law. She should remind herself of the question that should guide all of us when writing, editing, and evaluating personal statements: *Why does the candidate want to go to law school?*

Final Assessment

I am going to repeat my advice from earlier in this review, because it captures the essence of what is wrong with this essay and highlights where the candidate should start her revisions: "Curse only sparingly, disparage your present-day self even more sparingly, and in general, avoid dramatic tales of romance." After a solid rewrite based on this guidance, the candidate could turn her attention to more specific matters—such as some of the overly abstract phrasings and the clarification of her interest in the law—but not until then.

Personal Statement 49

Be sparing with
absolute language.

Everyone said it would be a mistake to keep my baby. My mother, my father, my teachers, my guidance counselor. Seventeen when I got pregnant, I would not even have a chance to graduate high school before he was born. Instead of going to the prom, I'd be going to the maternity unit. Instead of putting on a cap and gown, I'd be putting diapers on another human being.

But the moment I first held my son, I knew I'd made the right decision. When he looked up at me with his huge blue eyes, I felt a determination born inside of me. I made a promise that this baby boy who everyone said would be a stumbling block in my path would really be a blessing. He would be a blessing by making me work harder than I ever had before to build the best possible life I could for both of us.

Up until that point, I hadn't worked so hard at anything. I rarely went to school, blowing off classes to hang out and smoke pot with my friends. I went to parties most nights of the week, often with the older kids who'd finished or dropped out of high school and were doing nothing with their lives but that listless hanging out. The guy who'd gotten me pregnant was someone I'd met exactly twice, whose last name I wasn't even sure of. When I told him, he asked me if my parents would pay for the abortion if I just said I didn't know whose the baby was.

When Michael was born, all of that changed in the blink of an eye. At first, making a better life for the two of us meant getting a job and getting out of my parent's house. Luckily, they were still around to help watch him while I worked long shifts at the Gap. I rarely slept. I would come home from work, feed Michael, take a nap, and be up again shortly thereafter to change him.

After Michael and I got settled in our new life, I decided to get my GED. I studied in the back room on my breaks and on my days off. I passed with flying colors and was on to my next challenge—community college. It was difficult, sometimes, taking classes with people years younger than me. They had lives that I couldn't imagine anymore. But many of them did not have the drive I had to succeed. At the end of my first semester, my grades reflected that drive. I had a 3.9 average.

While my fellow students wrote for newspapers and played sports, I took my son to daycare and folded shirts in rectangles. While other people at school complained about having to wake up at seven a.m., I wondered if I'd ever sleep again. And through it all, I watched the big blue eyes of my little baby boy get bluer and deeper and wider, and I knew I would go for the rest of my life without sleep if I had to.

I finished community college at age 25. My son was in first grade by then. Some people would have been happy there, would have felt that they had accomplished enough. With my degree, I could have gotten a job in an office, gotten health insurance and an IRA. But I had made my son that promise. So I started applying to four-year programs. My son and I became "homework buddies," doing our assignments together at the kitchen table at night.

I studied English, the thing I had always been best at in high school. Back then, I had loved writing poems. Now, I was set on doing something different. After college, I planned on going to law school. I knew that my skills with the written word would come in handy in a career as a lawyer.

Three more years passed. Michael was ten, but I still wasn't getting any sleep. Not content to just study, go to work, and raise a son, I had also begun interning at a local law firm. At my graduation from college, Michael sat in the audience and waved to me as I walked across the stage. I don't think I've ever been happier.

Once, when I was young and didn't know what I was getting myself into, people told me that having a baby would be a mistake. But as it turned out, having a child motivated me to do things that I hadn't even dreamed of before he came along. And now, at age 28, with my child growing and a bright future ahead of both of us, I am happy to have made mistakes, and used them to motivate me. Being a lawyer is the next step on the path to that future. Even if it means giving up sleep for a little while longer.

jdMission Review

Overall Lesson

Use extreme language only in extreme circumstances.

First Impression

I like how the candidate immediately introduces a difficult choice she had to make. We now know what to expect in her essay—we will hear about how she arrived at her decision or about what her life was like after she made it.

Strengths

This candidate strikes me as resilient, proactive, and persevering. She has made her own way—that is clear. She also tells her story without victimizing herself or appealing to the reader's sympathy, which is a surprisingly difficult task with this type of subject matter. I want her to succeed, and I actually believe that she will. What a powerful take-away!

Weaknesses

This might seem nitpicky, but extreme language can sound stale in personal statements. For those of us who read tons of them (and admissions officers read *many* more than I do), lines like this one feel a bit trite (note the extreme language, in bold): "He would be a blessing by making me **work harder than I ever had before** to build **the best possible life** I could for both of us."

What if the candidate had instead written, "He would make me work harder than I had been, because I wanted to build a good life for us both"? This sentence conveys the same idea without the grandiose language and, for some reason, is more powerful—perhaps because we often do not actually think in extremes; we just write about them in retrospect. The candidate probably did not actually think to herself, "I'm going to create the best possible life for us."

More than likely, her thought was something comparable but less absolute and less inherently competitive—something along the lines of "I'm going to create a good life for us."

Absolute statements also tend to sound more unreasoned than reasoned—and law school is all about reason. This is yet another argument for avoiding extreme language in personal statements.

Finally, the candidate maintains the same pace throughout her story from high school to present day, giving each phase equal attention and time, but some parts of her narrative are more important to her law school application than others and should therefore receive more consideration. For example, she could consolidate the details of her Gap job and her community college education into a smaller portion of the essay and focus more on her four-year program and law firm internship, given that those experiences and accomplishments will be most relevant to her aptitude for law school.

Final Assessment

Like most essays in the early-draft stage, this one could benefit first from a thorough edit to condense some areas and then the addition of new material to expand others. I would also encourage the candidate to scour her essay for any absolute terms (perhaps even marking them with a highlighter) and then to consider each one individually, asking herself, "Is this necessary? Is this true? Can I say this in a more tempered way?" Doing so—and eliminating any instances that do not truly enhance her story—will strengthen this already promising essay and result in a compelling personal statement.

PERSONAL STATEMENT 50

Ensure that your essay supports
the rest of your application.

50. Ensure that your essay supports the rest of your application.

When I was thirteen years old, after seven years of playing softball, I quit. I did so undramatically. My coach, tired of watching me fool around and pay little attention to what was going on around me, announced at the beginning of a game that I would be playing right field. If you don't know Little League or teens softball very well, right field is where the coaches put you when you can't catch and can't throw. It's where they hope you will do the least possible damage. I had been playing softball for seven years, and here I was playing the same position I started in at age six. I stood out in the field watching the game. I didn't even bother moving, not even when the ball came down the line between me and center field. I stood there for nine innings. When I walked home at the end of the game, I simply never went back. Not to practice, not to the next game, not to the end of the season party. I quit, as easy as that.

When I was a sophomore in high school, all my friends joined the soccer team. Dutifully, I went out and bought an Adidas duffel bag, shin guards, and soccer shoes. I had never played before, but I was determined to learn. I went to pre-season practice every day. I ran laps around the school football field along with the other girls (soccer required much more running than baseball). I did so many sit ups that muscles began to ripple across my abdomen. I ran drills. I learned how to pass and aim for the goal. I became so much better than I was when I started. When the lists got posted for first and second string, I was convinced that I would be on first, along with all my friends.

My friends made it. I did not.

I never went back to practice.

By the time I reached college, I had made a steady habit of quitting when things didn't go my way. And part way through my first semester, I had about had it with school. The classes were harder than the ones I had sailed through in high school, I was eating poorly and had gained quite a bit of weight, I was having a hard time keeping a budget, and, with my newfound freedom, I was drinking just a little too much—all pretty typical freshman problems. But to me, they seemed like the end of the world.

To make things worse, I had read Jean Paul Sartre's plays in high school and loved them so much that I thought taking a class where we read the entirety of *Being and Nothingness* would be a good idea. The class was killing me. Having never taken a philosophy class before, I couldn't follow the ideas behind existentialism. The other people in the class talked like they had been reading philosophy texts since grade school. I spent the first half of the semester asking questions that other students snickered at, and the second drawing in my notebook. I was going to fail. Better yet, I was going to quit before I failed.

I stopped going to the class. I missed one class; I felt better already. I missed two; this was clearly the right decision. I missed three; suddenly, in my inbox, there was an email from my professor asking if I was okay. When I emailed back, saying I was, he suggested that I come by his office and talk to him.

I probably could have avoided doing so, but I didn't. He was a nice guy, I thought. He tried really hard to be a good teacher. I guessed I owed him some sort of explanation.

I explained. I told him how I was having trouble understanding, how stupid the class made me feel. I confessed that the best way, it seemed, to avoid that feeling was not to show up at all.

He listened to me talk. He really was a good teacher. After I got done talking, he said, "Look, fine if you're never going to be a philosopher. But that doesn't mean you have to be a quitter."

Something clicked for me in that moment. I wasn't a baseball star, so I was a quitter. I wasn't first string in soccer, so I was a quitter. And I certainly wasn't a philosopher. But did I have to go on being a quitter?

If this were a movie, I'd have stayed in the class and gotten an A at the end. But I didn't.

I got a C+.

Over the next four years, I was faced with many more situations where the choices were be less than a star, or a quitter. And every time, I chose to stick with it. I learned the valuable trait of tenacity, a trait I think would serve me well in my professional future. As my quitting days fell further and further behind me, I began to excel in the things that I committed myself to, as you will see reflected in the grades I achieved in my last two years of college.

50. Ensure that your essay supports the rest of your application.

Now, I am confident that even if I am not always the star of something, I will complete it to best of my ability. When the choice comes down to quitting or finishing, I choose finishing.

JDMISSION REVIEW

Overall Lesson

Your personal statement should fit in well with the rest of your application.

First Impression

I like the first paragraph, and I like the candidate.

Strengths

This essay achieves something many others cannot: it focuses to a very significant degree on expressing the candidate's vulnerability (she devotes more than 80% of her personal statement to describing herself as a quitter) but then makes a meaningful and poignant 180-degree turn to transform her instances of quitting into a story about a powerful transition. By the end of the essay, I completely believe the candidate; I believe her transition from being a habitual quitter to making strong commitments to her endeavors was real (and as she notes, I can refer to her transcript to confirm this)—but more importantly, I believe *in* her. She has sunk, she has reflected, and she has risen. Many candidates attempt to write about this type of arc, but few do so convincingly, and fewer still do so as powerfully as this individual has.

Weaknesses

The question of whether to discuss your decision to attend law school in your personal statement is contentious. Notice that this essay does not address the candidate's reasons for wanting to attend law school at all.

Here is my general advice on this issue: if the rest of your application does not clearly indicate why you are applying—say, for example, you have no legal internship or student group experience, majored in a subject unrelated to law, and spent the past five years working in a biology lab—then you should at least touch on your reasons for pursuing a law degree in your personal statement.

However, if your application already demonstrates why you are applying to law school—whether through your college extracurricular activities, your work history, or your coursework—then you are probably safe to submit a personal statement that does not directly mention law school. I am *not* saying you *should* avoid discussing your law school aspirations in your essay, but in this case, if the candidate's resume and/or transcript clearly communicate her interest in the law, I think this type of essay is acceptable.

Finally, this essay is on the long side, so it needs to be shortened a bit. Specifically, I would suggest removing any expendable text from her discussion of her quitting habit. However, she should *add* a few examples of times when she "was faced with many more situations where the choices were be less than a star, or a quitter" and yet chose to "stick with it." This can be accomplished in a single sentence; she does not need to get too detailed or belabor the points.

Final Assessment

I would discuss with the candidate how this essay fits in with the rest of her application. If her overall application is strong (and, specifically, reflects why she wants to go into law), I would feel comfortable with her submitting this personal statement with only minor editorial tweaks.

INDEX

M7 FINANCIAL

RIGHT LOAN.
CAREER **ADVANTAGE.**

Refinance Your Student Loans and Save!
You may be able to save a significant amount of money by quickly and easily refinancing your federal and private student loans.

Competitively Priced Student Loans (No Origination Fees!)
Check out competitively priced student loans for law, MBA, medicine, graduate, and undergraduate programs.

Exclusive Graduate Program Ratings & Much More
Discover complimentary program ratings, career primers, educational guides, and a career coaching session.

You can access all this and more at www.m7financial.com.

How we're different:

SIMPLY THE BEST INSTRUCTORS

Everyone says they have the best, but we have the highest compensation in the industry. No sliding scale – we hire only experts, so our students are assured the best. 99th-percentile scores and two years of teaching experience are required just to get an interview, and we hire only 2% of these qualified applicants.

CLASS THAT FEELS LIKE TUTORING

Why do we hire the best? So we have the talent needed to make every class session tailored to each student. Our capped classes ensure you get plenty of interaction with the instructor, and our flexible materials and LSAT experts ensure that each lesson is unique and tailored to your class.

TEACHING DOESN'T STOP
AT THE CLASSROOM DOOR

You can't be in the classroom every day, but you should have access to instructors even after you leave. We pay our instructors to respond to your questions between classes, and each student receives weekly, one-on-one office hours sessions.

SEE FOR YOURSELF WITH A FREE SESSION!

www.manhattanprep.com/lsat/classes/free/

jdMission gives you the competitive edge you need to get into the law school of your dreams.

Our team of experienced Senior Consultants is committed to helping you create an application that will dazzle the admissions committees and set you apart from the rest of the candidate pool.

Free 30-Minute Consultation

Visit www.jdmission.com/consult to start getting answers to all your law school application and admissions questions!

jdMission Resources

Check out our blog at www.jdmission.com/blog for personal statement advice and reviews, JD news, professor profiles, law school facts, and other valuable information!

jdMission Services

Whether you are looking for help finessing your personal statement, revamping your resume or just want a final "sanity check" on your completed application, jdMission is here for you!

jdMission

🌐 www.jdmission.com   ✉ info@jdmission.com